First World War
and Army of Occupation
War Diary
France, Belgium and Germany

14 DIVISION
Divisional Troops
25 Sanitary Section
21 May 1915 - 31 March 1917

WO95/1892/2

The Naval & Military Press Ltd
www.nmarchive.com
Published in association with The National Archives

Published by

The Naval & Military Press Ltd

Unit 10 Ridgewood Industrial Park,

Uckfield, East Sussex,

TN22 5QE England

Tel: +44 (0) 1825 749494

www.naval-military-press.com

www.nmarchive.com

This diary has been reprinted in facsimile from the original. Any imperfections are inevitably reproduced and the quality may fall short of modern type and cartographic standards.

© **Crown Copyright**
Images reproduced by permission of The National Archives, London, England, 2015.

Contents

Document type	Place/Title	Date From	Date To
Heading	1892/2		
Heading	14th Division 25th Sanitary Section May 1915-1917 Mar To 2 Army		
Heading	14th Division Summarised But Not Capied 25th Sanitary Section Vol I 21/5-31/5/17		
War Diary	Aldershot	21/05/1915	21/05/1915
War Diary	Southampton	22/05/1915	22/05/1915
War Diary	Le Havre	23/05/1915	23/05/1915
War Diary	Watten	24/05/1915	24/05/1915
War Diary	Watten (Le Mont)	25/05/1915	26/05/1915
War Diary	Zuytpeene	27/05/1915	27/05/1915
War Diary	Steenvoorde	28/05/1915	29/05/1915
War Diary	Westoutre	30/05/1915	31/05/1915
Heading	14th Division 25th Sanitary Section Summarised But Not Copied Vol II June 1915		
Heading	War Diary Of 25th Sanitary Section From 1st June 1915 to 30th June 1915 Volume I		
War Diary	Westoutre	01/06/1915	13/06/1915
War Diary	Hillhoek	14/06/1915	22/06/1915
War Diary	Vlamertinghe	23/06/1915	30/06/1915
Miscellaneous	14th (Light) Division Appendix No.1	12/06/1915	12/06/1915
Miscellaneous	14th (Light) Division Appendix II	13/06/1915	13/06/1915
War Diary	To The ADMS Con Appendix II	13/06/1915	13/06/1915
Heading	14th Division. 25th Sanitary Section Vol III Summarised But Not Copied July 15		
Heading	War Diary Of 25th Sanitary Section R.A.M.C.T. From 1st July 1915 to 31st July 1915 (Volume I)		
War Diary	Vlamertinghe	01/07/1915	31/07/1915
Heading	14th Division Summarised But Not Copied 25th Sanitary Section Vols 4, 5, 6 Aug Sept to Oct 15		
Heading	War Diary Of 25th Sanitary Section From 1st August 1915 to 31st August 1915 (Volume 4)		
War Diary	Vlamertinghe	01/08/1915	31/08/1915
War Diary	War Diary Of 25th Sanitary Section From 1st September 1915 To 30th September 1915 Volume 5		
War Diary	Vlamertinghe	01/09/1915	30/09/1915
War Diary	War Diary Of 25th Sanitary Section From 1st October 1915 To 31st October 1915 Volume 6		
War Diary	Vlamertinghe	01/10/1915	31/10/1915
Heading	14th Division Summarised but not copied 25th San. Sect. Vol 7 Nov 15		
Heading	War Diary Of 25th Sanitary Section. From 1st November to 30th November 1915 (Vol I)		
War Diary	Vlamertinghe	01/11/1915	30/11/1915
Heading	14th Div Summarised but not copied 25th San Sect. Vol 8 December 1915		
Heading	War Diary Of 25th Sanitary Section R.A.M.C.T. From 1st December 1915 To 31st December 1915 (Volume) 1		
War Diary	Vlamertinghe	01/12/1915	31/12/1915
Miscellaneous	Nominal Roll	20/12/1915	20/12/1915

Heading	14th San Sect 25 Vol 9 Jan 1916		
War Diary	Vlamertinghe	01/01/1916	31/01/1916
Heading	14th Div. 25th Sany Section Feb 1916		
Heading	San Sect 25 Vol 10		
War Diary	Vlamertinghe	01/02/1916	12/02/1916
War Diary	Esquelbecq	13/02/1916	18/02/1916
War Diary	Flesselles	19/02/1916	23/02/1916
War Diary	Doullens	24/02/1916	24/02/1916
War Diary	Sus. St. Leger.	25/02/1916	28/02/1916
War Diary	Barly	29/02/1916	29/02/1916
Heading	14th Div 25 San Sec Vol II March 1916		
War Diary	Barly	01/03/1916	01/03/1916
War Diary	Borneville	02/03/1916	06/03/1916
War Diary	Barly	01/03/1916	01/03/1916
War Diary	Borneville	02/03/1916	16/03/1916
War Diary	Warlus	17/03/1916	31/03/1916
Heading	War Diary Of 25th Sanitary Section For April 1916 14 Div		
War Diary	Warlus	01/04/1916	30/04/1916
Heading	War Diary Of 25th Sanitary Section R.A.M.C.T. (T.F.) From 1st May 1916 To 31st May 1916 25 San Sec Vol 13		
War Diary	Warlus	01/05/1916	31/05/1916
Heading	No. 25 San. Sect June 1916		
War Diary	Warlus	01/06/1916	30/06/1916
Heading	15th Division 25th Sanitary Section July 1916		
War Diary	Warlus	01/07/1916	29/07/1916
War Diary	Sus. St Leger	30/07/1916	30/07/1916
War Diary	Frohen Le Grand. (Frohen-Le-Petit)	31/07/1916	31/07/1916
Heading	14th Div no. 25 Sanitary Section August 1916		
War Diary	Bernaville. (Somme)	01/08/1916	06/08/1916
War Diary	Near. Buire-Sur-L'Encre.	07/08/1916	12/08/1916
War Diary	BelleVille Farm. (S.E. of Albert)	13/08/1916	30/08/1916
War Diary	Belloy. (W. of Amiens)	31/08/1916	31/08/1916
Heading	14th (light) Div No.25 Sanitary Section Sept 1916		
War Diary	Belloy	01/09/1916	10/09/1916
War Diary	Near. Buire-Sur-L'Encre.	11/09/1916	12/09/1916
War Diary	Fricourt Chateau	13/09/1916	16/09/1916
War Diary	Near Buire-Sur-L'Encre	17/09/1916	21/09/1916
War Diary	Le Cauroy	22/09/1916	25/09/1916
War Diary	Gouy. Warlus.	26/09/1916	27/09/1916
War Diary	Warlus.	28/09/1916	30/09/1916
Heading	14th Div 25th Sanitary Section. Oct. 1916		
War Diary	Warlus	01/10/1916	26/10/1916
War Diary	Le Cauroy.	27/10/1916	31/10/1916
Heading	War Diary Of 25th Sanitary Section For Month Of November 1916		
War Diary	Le Cauroy.	01/11/1916	30/11/1916
Heading	14th Div 25th Sanitary Section. War Diary. For Period-December 1 to 31, 1916 Vol 20		
War Diary	Le Cauroy.	01/12/1916	18/12/1916
War Diary	Warlus.	19/12/1916	31/12/1916
Heading	14th Div, 25th Sanitary Section. Jan 1917		
War Diary	Warlus	01/01/1917	31/01/1917
Heading	War Diary Of OC 25th Sanitary Section For month of February. Vol 22		

War Diary	Warlus	01/02/1917	28/02/1917
Heading	14th Div. no. 25 Sanitary Section. mar 1917		
War Diary	Warlus	01/03/1917	31/03/1917

14TH DIVISION

25TH SANITARY SECTION

MAY 1915 - ~~DEC 1916~~
 497 MAR

To 2. ARMY

/g/ 14th Division

12/5/444

12.1/5/444

Summarised but not copied

25th Sanitary Section

Vol I

21/5/ - 31/5/75

May 1915

Ans

Army Form C. 2118.

2nd Sanitary Sec'n 14th Div.

WAR DIARY
or
INTELLIGENCE SUMMARY.
(Erase heading not required.)

Instructions regarding War Diaries and Intelligence Summaries are contained in F. S. Regs., Part II. and the Staff Manual respectively. Title pages will be prepared in manuscript.

Place	Date	Hour	Summary of Events and Information	Remarks and references to Appendices
ALDERSHOT	1915 May 21	7 am	Motor Lorry of Corpl Bailey left for SOUTHAMPTON and 11-30 a.m. Entrained with vehicles 1-30 p.m.	
		10-50	Sec'n left Blackdown, ALDERSHOT entrained and started 0-55 p.m.	
		3.0 p.m	SOUTHAMPTON disembarked and Sec'n complete by 4 p.m. 55 transchars	
		4.30 p.m	left Quay transchart in SOUTHAMPTON WATER	
SOUTHAMPTON	22	4.3 p.m	SOUTHAMPTON	
LE HAVRE	23	4.30 a.m	Arrived LE HAVRE and disembarked	
		6.20 p.m	left by train with A.A.R Field Ambulance	
WATTEN	24	5.0 p.m	and St Omer	
		5.30 p.m	Marched to WATTEN. Billeted with 44 & 3 A at Le Mont	
WATTEN (LE MONT)	25		Sec'n dug three pit constructed Petrohn Pendes Incinerate Grease Trap & Tester Seater.	
		9.30 AM	Men inspected Billets with 44 & 7A San Officer. Requested Billets to be cleaned	
			out. They cleaned thoroughly, 7 Sprayed with Cresol. Bedding taken 250-300 men were sleeping	
			ordered by means of horses Cadder through transport new Cadder O.S.P. Old Cadder O.S.P. returned Town &	
			inhabitants Latrines put Old Beannes.	
		3 pm	Marched men to new billets in company with Interpreter. Inspector found Billets	
			most unsanitary, tequile inspected & accommodate men. Otherwen permission from D.A.D.M.S. & to muster new LE MONT	

1577 Wt. W.10791/1773 500,000 1/15 D. D. & L. A.D.S.S./Forms/C. 2118.

25th Sanitary Section 14th Div.

Army Form C. 2118.

WAR DIARY
or
INTELLIGENCE SUMMARY.
(Erase heading not required.)

Instructions regarding War Diaries and Intelligence Summaries are contained in F.S. Regs., Part II. and the Staff Manual respectively. Title pages will be prepared in manuscript.

Place	Date	Hour	Summary of Events and Information	Remarks and references to Appendices
WATTEN (LE MONT)	1915 May 26	10 A.M.	Men marched out 2 rooms after our 43rd F.A.	
		2.0 P.M.	Lab[ourer]s to Section by O.C. on Fly Nuisance, prevention thereof.	
		5.25	Rec'd instructions from D.A.D.M.S. to proceed LE DERZEELE to join 43rd F.A. marched here in eve.	
ZUYTPEENE	27	7.0 A.M.	Marched and 43rd F.A. to ZUYTPEENE. Halted to rest. Taken Tech'l Supply, of Billets, Water. Billets required 2nd H.Q. Supply, no Red Crossing near guide. Supr Men. Construction Sanitary arrangements.	
STEENVOORDE	28	8.0 A.M.	Section marched to STEENVOORDE went into Billets.	
		5.0 P.M.	Boy Scout Paton Conveyed to Northminster R.A. Temporary Hospital by order D.A.D.M.S.	
STEENVOORDE	29	10.0 A.M.	Sergt. Hazell, Ptes. Mackay, Heard, Read, Overton joined 42nd F.A. at SYLVESTRE. Cpl. Bailey, Ptes Rid. Hollis, Clark & Finch joined 43rd F.A. at CAESTRE. Ptes Mackintosh inspected camp of 14th L? Hughes Mos??? Palmer inspected and camps Dog struck L.S. Ptes Kemsher & Fryer inspected all camps Dog Struck L.?	
STEENVOORDE			under instructions from D.A.D.M.S.	
WESTOUTRE	30	6.0 A.M.	Marched to WESTOUTRE (environs of Scalin) arr 11.0 A.M. Generally inspected Sanitation of Village.	
DO.	31	8.0 A.M.	Took over Sanitation from Sanitary Section 3rd Div. Section worked on cleaning of Town etc. Where men working & Res.	
			Cpl visited LA CLYTTE and D.A.D.M.S. inspected rooms used for Bathing.	
		2.30 P.M.	Sgt Hazell & Ptes. MacKay, Heard & Allen despatched to DICKE BUSH to supervise the Method of EFA:	
			Ye 2nd visit to LA CLYTTE inspected Drinking Water. Source of this partly completed.	

Brockelbe Lieut
Ramst

121/5871.

121/5871
14/4/15 P.W recd

5/
June 1915
Summarised but not copied 25th Sanitary Section.
Vol: II

Confidential

War Diary

of

25th Sanitary Section

from 1st June 1915 to 30th June 1915

Volume I

Army Form C. 2118.

WAR DIARY
or
INTELLIGENCE SUMMARY
(Erase heading not required.)

Place	Date	Hour	Summary of Events and Information	Remarks and references to Appendices
WESTOUTRE	1915 June 1		All roads swept, rubbish carted to incinerator, household refuse collected & destroyed with 29 fatigue men & 4 horses supplied by 42nd F.A. Several samples Malsterkerke at WESTOUTRE. At LA CLYTTE Corpl Bailey & 7 men inspected & took source of running insanitary conditions of R.A.M.C. field OC visited LA CLYTTE & DICKEBUSCH on a tour of inspection. DICKEBUSCH Sanitation attended to by Sergt Hazell & squad.	
DO	2		O.C. Twice visited LA CLYTTE & DICKEBUSCH & inspected Baths, Lake & Cemetery, arranged for fatigue parties & Corpl Bailey inspected C & D Camps & Som. L.I. Found in good condition the Corpl & inspanning Camps 14th Heavy Battery RCA & 100th Coy A.S.C. 1st & 4th Aun Col. Sgt Imuells squad continuing inspection DICKEBUSCH Sidwick, WESTOUTRE Sanitation attended to.	
DO	3		O.C. visited HAZEBROUCK & ST OMER with DADMS re search of Baths for Bathoeke Sgt Hazell & squad at DICKEBUSCH arranged with Camp Comm and out for fatigue men re personal sanitation generally. Attempt to Bacon & two medicated entrains made of Trench typhus Corpl Bailey consulted with MO. at LACLYTTE re water supply warning of Pte Clark to test same kept am method of filtration & force of R.A.M.C. 43rd F.A. App. 23 men re Horses supplies by H2um F.A.	
DO	4		WESTOUTRE roads cleaned rubbish disposed of. Acres of meals & of refuse disinfected (Removed clothing) Temporary Public Cature constructed (Poles procured with Handsaw) 2 Boiles fitted & Baths ArA. O.C. visited MOUNT NOIR Private Hospital & complained by Staff Sergt FULLER re respects & fuelings. O.C. consulted by Col Prentice C.R.E. on Trench Shelters for men purchasing against morning gases	
DO	5	2.30	O.C. accompanied C. 42nd F.A. Received on tour Survey of Water supply for C.A.L. Paid visit in evening & usual round taken. Carried out by Section.	

WAR DIARY
or
INTELLIGENCE SUMMARY
(Erase heading not required.)

Army Form C. 2118.

D.S.A Sanitary Section

25th SANITARY SECTION
R.A.M.C.(T.)

Place	Date	Hour	Summary of Events and Information	Remarks and references to Appendices
WESTOUTRE	1915 June 6		O.C. visited various camps in neighbourhood of DICKEBUSCH & also visited Horse F.A. on road between in reservoir. Kind permission carried out at LACLYTTE & WESTOUTRE	
Do	7		O.C. visited Advanced R.F.A. Ammn Col & inspector camp of A.D.S. Inspection engine of HAZEBROUCK bi-carms disinfector & Barlow also Water M/N air hospital. Inspected improvement in water taps & marvoirs camps on LA CLYTTE & DICKEBUSCH districts in enjoiner condition.	
Do	8		O.C. visited Canada South & Camp, Dismendin at DROMBUSCH & pard further visit HAZEBROUCK in connection with purchase of Boilers	
Do	9		O.C. Visited Water Source at LA CLYTTE in company with O.C. 144 F.A. reconnoitred dug in LACLYTTE neighbourhood. Inspected MMG Camp anryers for improvements 1st made near of Section engaged inspecting chicks in DICKEBUSCH & LACLYTTE Area & improving Sanitation	WESTOUTRE
Do	10	9 am	Corporal BAILEY promoted to Lce Sergt. Lce Corporal SIMPSON to Acting Corporal also KIRK, HEATHER, HEATH & HOLLIS to Lce Corporals. All these promotions without extra pay. O.C. inspected 42nd F.A. at LOCRE Inspected Reservoir & men filter Section man reserving. Sanitation course at LACLYTTE & DICKEBUSCH & WESTOUTRE poke workshop parties.	
Do	11	9.0	O.C. visited Trenches beyond DICKEBUSCH & found Sanitation held back for want of drainpipe & cesspit near of Section inspecting crinde in area. Stacking water. Water generally near pool during the last few days owing to heavy downpour of rain preventing troops the heavy manner	See Appendix No 7.

WAR DIARY or INTELLIGENCE SUMMARY

Army Form C. 2118.

25th Sanitary Section
14th Division

Place	Date	Hour	Summary of Events and Information	Remarks and references to Appendices
	1915			
WESTOUTRE	11		Rand with Water Supplies, mostly drawn from shallow wells. Corpm. Simpson detailed to trenches beyond DICKEBUSCH attached to 7th R.B. to supervise sanitation for 48 hours.	
Do	12	9.30	O.C. engaged all morning with D.A.D.M.S. and Chief Supply Officer discussing Supplies Disinfectants in Trenches which have hitherto been inadequate. AAA. Arrangements made for disinfecting the supply of Chloride Lime.	
Do			Sanitation at WESTOUTRE mostly carried out by our own men AAA. Local appeals to Army experience in procuring fatigues for sanitary work. The Division only just counts into a home there has been no opportunity to weed out unefficients from the Infantry Units AAA. Civilian labour is fully employed mending roads & working in the fields. To engage with civilian labour.	
Do	Sunday 13	2.30	Sanitation at WESTOUTRE carried out by our own squad in absence of fatigue party. 42nd F.A. keen workers.	
Do	"	9.15	R. engaged all morning experimenting with C.R.E. on apparatus for counteracting the effects of Chlorine Gas	See Appendix II
		2.30	O.C. visited LACLYTTE saw O.C. 46th F.A. re newly prepared Entering Brave-themes A.S.C. see Appendix No 2.	
HILLHOEK	14	9.30	Marched to HILLHOEK 20th Divisional Hts. to await "unit" camp there. Settled with Mayor of WESTOUTRE re Billeting	
Do		2.30	Arranged Camp Sanitation for Air N°200	
Do	15		Sgt HAKELL + 6 men + Sgt BAILEY + 6 men marched thurdy night from DICKEBUSCH + LACLYTTE respects. Found section the end of the mom. O.C. re arranged Labine accomodation at H2 2h0 Camp	

WAR DIARY or INTELLIGENCE SUMMARY

Army Form C. 2118.

25 Sanitary Section
14th Division

Place	Date	Hour	Summary of Events and Information	Remarks and references to Appendices
HILLHOEK	June 15 1915	11.15	O.C. visited D.L. Dun Yermany, AAA. Camp well looked after, then visited 44th F.A. at SCHOUDENONTHOEK. Inspected reconvalescent tent tent. Men engaged on sanitation for the 2hrs Camp.	
Do.	,, 16		O.C. rode out beyond WATOU in endeavour to find Good Water Supply. Then J Section engaged inspecting various Camps in vicinity of Hd. 2hrs.	
Do.	,, 17		O.C. visited Barking Dog Farm. Trapped many Stream on boundary. Fine 2 Regiment Tr. Supply looked at place. Lce Cpl Simpson fetched Thead Disinfector from Creek. Rest f Section inspected Camps moderated place.	
Do.	,, 18	MORN	O.C. visited VLAMERTINGHE with Col Tanner & ADMS, and work argent at MAULE & occasional water Supply in new area. Sergts HAXELL, BAILEY, Corpl SIMPSON Pte Ls Corps HEATH, HOLLIS, Ptes MACKAY, SMITH, CLARK, ODDEN, HATTON, MEAD & FLINT went to new camps near VLAMERTINGHE in comection with sanitation in new area.	
		AFT	O.C. visited VLAMERTINGHE again with A.C. A.D.M.S. & the D.A.D.M.S. in search of room for baths. Also visited 42nd F.A. Dressing Station. Sgt HAXELL Hands engaged refurnishing Hd 2hrs Camp in new area.	
Do.	19		O.C. went into YPRES to inspect before entering Generals Funerals Advanced Hd 2hrs. Sanitation in new area approved by AcadvSection. Clothing from Kennes Scabies. 42 F.A. drawing Sh Sprayer with formulin.	
	20		O.C. visited VLAMERTINGHE on tour of inspection also 44 F.A. & arrangs for Thead Dernfector to be fried at their Camp for the time being under supervision of Pte PALMER.	

25 Sanitary Section
1st Division

WAR DIARY or INTELLIGENCE SUMMARY

Army Form C. 2118.

Place	Date	Hour	Summary of Events and Information	Remarks and references to Appendices
	1915			
HILLEHOEK	June 20	2.30	Corpl PEPPER, L/Corpl HEATHER and Pte KEITH, ROGERS, McCOY & MARS HALL proceeded to YPRES in conjunction with disposing of great quantity of refuse there.	
Do	21		OC all day at VLAMERTINGHE in connection Sanitation. 142rd Camp in advance here. Sgt HAXELL & party carrying out the work. Corpl PEPPERS squad disposing of refuse in YPRES. PSS FULLER & squad superintending at HILLEHOEK to see that Hd Qrs Camp there left in Sanitary condition. Corpl SIMPSON & Pte PALMER proceeded to 4 & 4 FA Rest Camp to instruct men in use of Thresh incinerator.	
Do	22	9.30	SS. FULLERS squad moved up to Hd Qrs Camp near YLAMERTINGHE	
		to		
		2.	OC visited YPRES re Sanitation of advance Hd Qrs. Corpl PEPPERS squad engaged there. After Rest Section engaged in Hd Qrs Camp which had been left in very unlidy condition.	
VLAMERTINGHE	23	MORN	OC took Sgt HAXELL & 7 men to work in manyards & Town of YPRES. Corpl SIMPSON & Pte FILKINS attached to 4 2nd FA to Trenches to supervise Sanitation.	
		AFTN	OC Survey of Section engaged at Hd Qrs Camps. Sgt BAILEY inspected Camps 7 & 8 & KRR & 7 & 8 KRB & found on the whole Camps in good condition.	
Do	24		OC examined Hell pond in Brickfield VLAMERTINGHE. read DADMS to water Sanitary officer 3rd Division. Sgt HAXELL & party engaged on disposal Refuse at YPRES. HSS FULLER visited YPRES to examine new Latrine. Corpl SIMPSON & Pte FILKINS arrested in trenches but released again after satisfaction being given they were bonafides.	

25th Sanitary Section
14th Division

WAR DIARY
or
INTELLIGENCE SUMMARY.
(Erase heading not required.)

Army Form C. 2118.

Place	Date	Hour	Summary of Events and Information	Remarks and references to Appendices
	1915			
VLAMERTINGHE	June 25		O.C. visited trenches beyond YPRES with D.A.D.M.S. on a visit of inspection AAA Sgt HAXELL'S party still engaged in YPRES preparing Grounds Hd qurs for reinforced Refuse AAA SS Fuller Spark Superintendent Sanitation Div Hdqtrs	
Do	June 26	Night	Corpl SIMPSON & Pte FILKINS attached to Advanced Dressing Station, Ecole de BIENFAISANCE.	
Do	June 26		O.C. visited Baths at POPPERINGHE reopened with Capt KAYE in disposal, saw lorry wrks etc Sector lorry (KARRIER) Steering gear broken – visits Supply Col. Sgt HAXELL'S party still engaged in YPRES. Rest of unit superintending Sanitation in camps in vicinity Div Hq Hts. It has been more difficult to keep Camps in a good Sanitary state owing to the heavy rainstorms during the week are the nature of the Sub-Soil.	
Do	Sunday June 27	Morn	O.C. inspected 4 Battalions in OUDERDOM wood & huts at Brickfields.	
Do		AFT	O.C. went to HAZEBROUCK in endeavour to obtain iron for spare part Lorry. Disposal Refuse Still going on in YPRES Sanitation work at Hd.Qtrs supervised. Corpl SIMPSON & Pte FILKINS with fatigue party thoroughly cleaned up Courtyard & Vicinity of Advanced Dressing Station at Ecole de BIENFAISANCE. Pails at N'yd the place was sheltered & burnt out, & they returned to Hd.Qtrs.	
Do	June 28	Morn	O.C. visited 7th K.R.R. & R.B. Transports also 43rd Batt. Transport, suggested various improvements in Sanitation AAA	
		AFT	O.C. visited new Area & started to do reconnaissance with C.R.E. AAA YPRES refuse disposal continued & Hd qtrs Sanitation supervised by unit.	

Army Form C. 2118.

WAR DIARY
or
INTELLIGENCE SUMMARY.
(Erase heading not required.)

Place	Date	Hour	Summary of Events and Information	Remarks and references to Appendices
	1915			
VLAMERTINGHE	Jun 29	9.30	Sgt HAXELL and party returned fm YPRES AAA. O.C. engaged all day inspecting rear area and water reconnaissance. Corpl PEPPER began finishing up disposal refuse YPRES ramparts + rear of unit inspecting camps nr VLAMERTINGHE AAA	
Do	Jun 30		O.C. visited HILLEHOEK & enquire into cases of suspected ENTERIC in 9th KRR AAA Also visited No 1 Mobile Laboratory 10th Casualty Clearing Station in consultation with O.C. Same and the D.A.D.M.S. Inspected camps in rear Area conducted water reconnaissance with DADMS. rear of units engaged loading units just moved into new area AAA. E Moskilth	

(Copy) Appendix No 1

To the A.D.M.S.
14th (Light) Division
From O.C.
25 Sanitary Section

Sir,
I have the honour to report that I made yesterday a personal inspection of the trenches and posted there a Sanitary Corporal to remain and supervise the general sanitary arrangements. AAA

The trenches inspected are held at the moment by the K.R.Rs and the 7th R.B who are working hard to remedy the extremely bad conditions they found on taking them over from the 86th Bde. AAA. These troops left latrine buckets and urine tubs full to overflowing and the ground in their neighbourhood in a filthy condition AAA

In certain places decomposing dead bodies are exposed in the walls and the stench from these is very offensive AAA. They should be well sprinkled with Chloride of Lime and covered with earth AAA

The use of earth in latrine buckets is impracticable, a supply of Chloride of Lime should be kept in each latrine enclosure and a little of the powder sprinkled over

25th SANITARY SECTION
No. 1
Date 12.6.15
R.A.M.C. (T.)

To the A.D.M.S. Cont'd.   Appendix No 1.

all fresh excreta AAA This would greatly minimise smell and also keep away the flies which swarm over the exposed faeces

Sanitary arrangements are now being properly carried out, but the sanitary squads are greatly hampered by a shortage of disinfectants, indents for which I was given to understand, had been sent in AAA The materials had not however been supplied in anything like the quantities asked for and required AAA

This is a matter which should be immediately attended to as it is absolutely essential that an adequate supply of disinfectants should be always available in the trenches, in view of the hot weather and the circumscribed space in which the men have to live and work

I have the honour to be Sir,
Your obedient Servant.
(Sd) E. Brooke Pike Lieut
R.A.M.C.T.
Commanding 25th Sanitary Section

12th June '15

(Copy) Appendix II

To the A.D.M.S.
14th (Light) Division

[Stamp: 25th SANITARY SECTION, No. II, Date 13.6.15, R.A.M.C. (T)]

Sir,
I have the honour to report the result of my inquiries with reference to the case of suspected Enteric Driver Thomas A.S.C.

1. The man had been bivouacing in the open
2. Had supposedly been drinking only Chlorinated water.
3. Had not suffered with Diarrhoea
4. His blankets and the sacking of which his bivouac was constructed have been burnt.
5. He has been sent into Hospital at BAILLEUL for definite diagnosis
6. All possible contacts are being carefully watched.
7. The man had been twice inoculated before leaving England

With reference to 2. His drinking

Appendix II

To the A.D.M.S. cont

only Chlorinated water. This must be considered the weak spot for when men or their ~~companions~~ comrades are billeted in a village where every cottage contains a pump, it is obviously impossible to prevent promiscuous drinking, especially when the inhabitants are known to consume the pump water with impunity.

I would suggest that O.C. Units be instructed to periodically remind men of the extreme danger of drinking water which has not been previously Chlorinated.

I have the honour to be
Sir,
Your obedient Servant
(sd) E. Brooke Pitcheint
RAMC T

Commanding 25 Sanitary Sect.

13/6/15

amt

121/6242

107/6242

14th Division.

ADMS Sanitary Section.
War Diary Vol: III
Summarised but not copied

July '15

War Diary

of

25th Sanitary Section
R.A.M.C.T.

from

1st July 1915 to 31st July 1915.
(Volume I)

Army Form C. 2118.

XIV Division

Instructions regarding War Diaries and Intelligence Summaries are contained in F.S. Regs., Part II. and the Staff Manual respectively. Title pages will be prepared in manuscript.

WAR DIARY
or
INTELLIGENCE SUMMARY.
(Erase heading not required.)

[Stamp: 25th SANITARY SECTION R.A.M.C.]

Place	Date	Hour	Summary of Events and Information	Remarks and references to Appendices
VLAMERTINGHE	1915 July 1	MORN.	O.C. visited YPRES with Col. TURNER remainder of G.H.2 Staff on Sanitary inspection of streets and ramparts.	
		AFT.	O.C. visited YPRES again. Inspected work being done from morning inspection. Corp. PEPPER & grad. engaged in Sanitation work at ECOLE DE BIENFAISANCE. Corp. SIMPSON & SIMKINS inspecting Sanitation in Rest Area. Reinspection of engineer in trenches & all water supplies in Advanced Area.	
Do	July 2	MORN.	O.C. visited YPRES with A.A. & Q.M.G. Inspected progress of Sanitary work under Corp. PEPPER & Fatigue	
		AFTN.	O.C. with A.D.M.S. firing order to HORTFALL destructors. Reinspection of trenches and supplies.	
Do	July 3	MORN.	O.C. attended demonstration of spraying of Refuse to Apr. Inspector K.R.R. & R.B. camps & Engineer Corps Camps under S.M.O. being briefed & particulars prepared for Med. Board meeting A.M.	
Do	4		O.C. inspected XIV Div. Baths POPERINGHE. Disposal of rubbish still being carried out at YPRES. Inspected guide by next section.	
Do	5	MORN.	O.C. visited trenches beyond YPRES with D.A.D.M.S. on visit of inspection. Section inspecting units.	
Do	6	AFTN.	O.C. visited Adm. Area with D.A.D.M.S.	Do
Do	6	MORN.	O.C. attended meeting V Corps Sanitary Committee where various types Sanitary conveniences were approved recommended for use by units XIV Div. Ypres. Arranged photostats of these be conducted at Hutsb camp as a guide for units.	
	7	MORN.	O.C. attended adjourned meeting 5th Corps Sani. Committee.	

(P/9P)

Army Form C. 2118.

WAR DIARY
or
INTELLIGENCE SUMMARY

(Erase heading not required.)

XIV Division

Instructions regarding War Diaries and Intelligence Summaries are contained in F.S. Regs., Part II. and the Staff Manual respectively. Title pages will be prepared in manuscript.

Place	Date	Hour	Summary of Events and Information	Remarks and references to Appendices
VLAMERTINGHE	1915 July 7	Aft'n	OC in consultation with DADMS + Sanitary Officer 5th Corps	
Do	8	MORN	Inspected Sub section. (Sgt HAXELL lyc HEATH, Pte MEAD + ODDEN) h/3rd Bde Hdqrs for inspection units in support area after demonstration to them modification of Sanitary conveniences	
		AFTN	OC met Sanitary Officer III Div in consultation re exhibition of model approach	
Do	9		Suggest dispatching Sgt BAILEY + party to REST AREA (attached 41st Bde Hdqrs) + Sgt SIMPSON + party to YPRES (attached 42nd Bde Hdqrs) + Sgt HAXELL 43rd — Sgt HAXELL & 43rd men (three squads.) Sgt HAXELL 43rd men Sgt SIMPSON + 3men, Sgt BAILEY 4 3men will move into different areas with their respective Brigades in future. First demonstration to them modification of Sanitary conveniences.	
Do	10		OC Inspected Huts A+B. RENINGHELST — VLAMERTINGHE Road + arranges for fatigue parties to clear rubbish + render them fit for occupation	
Do	11		Pte visited YPRES with Sanitary Officer 2nd Div + inspected Salvage stores	
Do	12		Visited XIV Div Baths at POPERINGHE + inspected Jelpel Baths in course of construction	
Do	13		Pte Inspected Camps in SUPPORT AREA + demonstrated models sanitary conveniences to Hdq+06 various parties	
Do	14	MORN	Visited Hdqrs 42nd Bde YPRES with AA. + 2 MG + QA DMS + arranged for samples of water in trenches to be taken for analysis. Also zephers in front to be tested for metalliferious	

Army Form C. 2118.

XIV Division

WAR DIARY
or
INTELLIGENCE SUMMARY.
(Erase heading not required.)

Instructions regarding War Diaries and Intelligence Summaries are contained in F.S. Regs., Part II. and the Staff Manual respectively. Title pages will be prepared in manuscript.

Place	Date	Hour	Summary of Events and Information	Remarks and references to Appendices
VLAMERTINGHE	1915 July 14	Aftn	O.C. visited Motor Repair Workshops STEENVOORDE with DADMS & arranged for Water Cart pumps & cylinders to be inspected for use in the trenches	
	15		O.C. inspected R.E. & Camp 7 & F.A.	
			O.C. visited Chemical Laboratory HAZEBROUK with samples from MOATY Trenches YPRES. Water from Moat can be used after Chlorination – Steam not to be used.	
	16		O.C. visited 42nd Brigade with ADMS. on round of inspection.	
	17		TC. Spent day in collecting reports from each unit stamping Division	
	18		O.C. visited No 4 Mobile Laboratory HAZEBROUK with reference to work on Moat in trenches beyond YPRES.	
	19	Morn	T.C. inspected Camp 6 & R.E. An infirmary visited Baths POPERINGHE inspected Bacteria Bed. 1st Carbol Bed just completed – in use	
	20	Morn	Inspected 43rd Bde Transport Camps	
		Aftn	Demonstrated mobile Sanitary Convenience borrow bunks at Holebre	
	21		O.C. visited 41st Bde Area, Inspected his Train Hdqtrs with the view of making place suitable as winter. Arranged with R.E. all other arrangements for Hdqtrs Staffs & Demonstrates Sanitary appliances for various units	
	22		O.C. inspected Infantry Camps about to be vacated.	EMD

Army Form C. 2118.

WAR DIARY
or
INTELLIGENCE SUMMARY.
(Erase heading not required.)

Instructions regarding War Diaries and Intelligence Summaries are contained in F.S. Regs., Part II. and the Staff Manual respectively. Title pages will be prepared in manuscript.

Place	Date	Hour	Summary of Events and Information	Remarks and references to Appendices
VLAMERTINGHE	July 23	Afternoon	O.C. went round with Infantry Staff Capt. & selected sites for camps in new area N. of POPERINGHE + VLAMERTINGHE Road	
Do	July 24		O.C. attended Sanitary meeting at VII Corps H.Qrs. with A.D.M.S. + D.A.D.M.S.	
	25	Morn	O.C. inspected new camp sites in company with Bde Major & 2 M.S.	
		Aftn	Rode out with D.A.D.M.S. to 49th R.F.A. Amm Col. H.qrs which had been left in very insanitary condition by previous occupier.	
	26		O.C. went round new Area with Staff Capt. + selected sites for R.A. Troops beyond POPERINGHE	
	27	Morn	O.C. visited YPRES + inspected ramparts	
		Aftn	Inspected area for new camps	
	28		O.C. visited 4 Bn. Bde camps & H.qrs on a tour of inspection	
	29	Morn	O.C. inspected A.S.C. camps in company with O.C. Divisional Train	
		Aftn	Visited 3 Camps in Salford Area with reference to latrine buckets needed in trenches	
	30		Re inspected Motor Ambulance Workshops Mobile Veterinary Section & 14th D.A.C. in Read area.	
	31		Re visited Camps in Support Area Hdqtrs 42nd Bde. & XIV Divl Bakhs Discussed with O.C. Divl Bakhs the question of the destruction of Lice in men's clothing.	
		Evening	Inspected Camp taken over by No. 10 Y.C.L. from the 7th K.R.R.s by special request of latter.	

D. Brodie Rose Lieut
R.A.M.C.

121/75-18

11/5 Division

Summarized but not copied

25th Sanitary Section
vols 4, 5, 6

Aug, Sep 1 & Oct 15

Aug 1915
Sept
Oct

Ans

Confidential
War Diary
of
25th Sanitary Section

from 1st August 1915 to 31st August 1915
(Volume I) 4

E. Mooke Pike
Capt
R. A. M. C. T.
OC
25th Sanitary Section

Army Form C. 2118.

WAR DIARY
or
INTELLIGENCE SUMMARY.
(Erase heading not required.)

Instructions regarding War Diaries and Intelligence Summaries are contained in F. S. Regs., Part II. and the Staff Manual respectively. Title pages will be prepared in manuscript.

Place	Date	Hour	Summary of Events and Information	Remarks and references to Appendices
VLAMERTINGHE	1915 August Aug 1		O.C. engaged all day in Orderly Room writing report	
	Aug 2	MORN	O.C. attended meeting on location of water supplies in Divn. Arranged with Area Cmdg.	
			POPERINGHE to prepare map for water area	
		AFTN	Inspected Transport Camps 8 & 9. 4 KRR & Oxfd & Bucks L.I.	
	Aug 3	MORN	O.C. visited Lieut MAYLE of the water Patrol for information re water sources on G.2 Sheet 28	
		AFTN	O.C. visited Bettencourt VLAMERTINGHE to obtain information re water sources	
	4		O.C. inspected C.R.A. Camp at request of Staff Captain responsible re water Transport Camp from Rly.	
		AFTN	Saw Staff Sergeant Park, YPRES have ramparts properly cleared up from MENINGATE to LILLE GATE.	
	5		O.C. on visit through VLAMERTINGHE on water location arrr. Arranged with Cmdg. of Water Truck	
			& Well & Brickfield for chlorination of all water taken from that source including recharging tanks over every 4 days	
	6		O.C. visited REST AREA inspecting Bivl. Train A.S.C. Corps temps D.L.O.Y.I.	
	7		O.C. rode round Camp in Woods which Abve. Bde. are about to occupy. A36. Sheet 28.	
			Inspected 7th K.R.R. 8th K.R.R. & 7th & 8th R.B. camps. Tested re capacity of Well in Brickfield H.7 L.9 L. Sheet 28, roughly 1000 Gallons a day.	

Army Form C. 2118.

WAR DIARY or INTELLIGENCE SUMMARY.
(Erase heading not required.)

Place	Date	Hour	Summary of Events and Information	Remarks and references to Appendices
VLAMERTINGHE	1915 Aug 8		O.C. visited exhibition of models at 46th Divisional Sanitary Section. Heights engaged writing reports on sanitation.	
	9		O.C. inspected C.R.A. Camp & 42nd Bde Transport Lines & 1 Battalion 9th K.R.R. - Then to YPRES at night with D.A.D.M.S. Visited Prison & Asylum	
	10	MORN	Visit to C.R.E. for information with reference to Water Tanks at ZILLEBEKE Lake & ramparts YPRES. Rode out with A.D.M.S. to K.R.R. Battalion inspected new form of Shelter for carrying wounded along trenches	
		AFTN	Rode out with A.D.M.S. to camping grounds at A.30 Central Sheet 28 inspected Battalion of ROYAL Fus.	
	11		Sketched out scheme for sanitation of wounded Monuments. Submitted map & sketch of areas sought located in XIV Divisional Area to A.D.M.S	
	12		Visited WATOU inspected 26th M.V.S. of new ashes 40th Mounted Brigade & 2nd Div. respectively	
			with A.D.V.S	
	13		O.C. inspected camp ground by 1/31 Bde.	
	14		Made a thorough sanitary inspection of proposed Sir Sty for in small trees of POPERINGHE	
	15		Report work in mainly Room	
	16		Visited 8th K.R.R. Camp inspected. Old well gird discovered in G.4.d.2.2. Sheet 28. Inspected Transport Lines 43rd Bde Ypres Section & cleaning.	
	17		O.C. inspected Heights Camp complained of Camp Commandant of condition. Interviewed all N.C.O.s in charge of them & watched them coverwhen at Sanitary Section.	

1577 Wt. W10791/1773 500,000 1/15 D. D. & L. A.D.S.S./Forms/C. 2118.

WAR DIARY
or
INTELLIGENCE SUMMARY.
(Erase heading not required.)

Army Form C. 2118.

Place	Date	Hour	Summary of Events and Information	Remarks and references to Appendices
WAMERTINGHE	1915 AUG 18	Morn	OC reported on. Rushing Beds XIV Div Baths. Unwell cold. 2nd Rec Hosp. Rev PRODDEN who was sick. Acting Sergeant SIMPSON suffering from nervous breakdown.	
		Aftn	Interview with DADMS evacuated Sgt SIMPSON to the 42nd F.A. Hospital. Detailed Staff Sergt FULLER to replace him in charge of route attached to 2nd Rec Hosp.	
	19		OC visited well in G 4 d 2.2, returns of water, 590 gallons. Visited XIV Div Bath POPERINGHE to discuss disinfector with OC Baths. PRODDEN sick. Sent him to 2nd FA Hospital for a report on this condition.	
	20		OC rode out with DADMS inspected wood H 1 a proposed site for wash stand wells.	
	21		OC rode to well G 4 d 2.2 arranged with 2nd K.R.R. to had pulled J pump. Benchwebs. Models of sanitary appliances to stream curls.	
	22		Visit of 7 R.B. Transport camp to Sim road of Text stables interchange of our Back lock G 4 d 2.2.	
	23	Aftn	Visit from Staff Offr XII Corps Chambers Supervise to whom OC demonstrated models of sanitary appliances. OC rode to 7 R.B. Transport Camp close to POPERINGHE than old well pumped out.	

Army Form C. 2118.

WAR DIARY
or
INTELLIGENCE SUMMARY.
(Erase heading not required.)

Instructions regarding War Diaries and Intelligence Summaries are contained in F. S. Regs., Part II. and the Staff Manual respectively. Title pages will be prepared in manuscript.

Place	Date	Hour	Summary of Events and Information	Remarks and references to Appendices
VLAMERTINGHE	1915 Aug 24		OC again inspected dead well G4a 2.2 estimates yield at 450 to 500 galls per day. Recommenced another 1 Tank to storing supply ready for carts to fill from. Inspected Farm H1a is an ordinary steps necessary for water surrounding sanitary.	
	25		OC inspected Camps of DCLI & KOYLI & also new Waterhole being dug in KOYLI Camp. OC warned note coming from German lines near POTYZE to poisons & organic impurity.	
	26		OC visited 2nd F.A. in Rest Area to enquire about sick men, also visited Baths (X & Div) Tingrelas Reffefer Hospital	
	27		OC inspected dug outs & trenches on Canal Bank in KAA1E Salient visited Hugh's 2nd Bde in Ramparts YPRES by Sally Port & arranged fatigue party to dispose of rubbish in incinerators near church.	
	28		Inspected RFA in Rest Area visited 2nd Battn Sanitary Exhibition in BAILLEUL. Tour Corpl HEATHER & made sketch.	
	29		7 Sanitary Appliances. Engaged all day on Reports.	
	30		Attended Water Conference at Corps HQrs with AA & QMG. Tingvelerzen water Tanks one Well in G4d 2.2. Inspected Waterhole recently dug in KOYLI Camp. Yield of which is estimated by KOYLI as 100 galls per hour.	
	31		OC inspected Camps of OC 1 Bucks Battalion & Transport & KOYLI re Waterhole.	

Confidential.

War Diary

of

25th Sanitary Section

From 1st September 1915   To 30th September 1915.
Volume 5

E. Brooke Pike
Capt
 R.A.M.C.T.
 OC
25th Sanitary Section

WAR DIARY
or
INTELLIGENCE SUMMARY.

Army Form C. 2118.

Place	Date	Hour	Summary of Events and Information	Remarks and references to Appendices
VLAMERTINGHE	1915 SEP 1		O.C. Inspected lines and camps in Harrison Area	
	2		Inspected bivouac fields in area taken over from 6th Division in company with A.D.M.S HAZING & A.D.M.S	
	3		Inspected possible billets for Chaplains of 4th Division. Suggested 2 detainees. Went to see Holmwood in wood to meet R.E. Officer who failed to keep appt.	
	4		Rode with R.E. Officer to examine hut sites in urgent need in concentration of batteries to save quarrying	
	5		O.C. inspected Transport Camp D.C.L.I. & 47th B.a.C. & B.A.C.	
			Weekly Report rendered. D.C.L.I & K.O.Y.L.I Camp on Company with A.D.M.S	
	6		O.C. made an examination of farm in Rest Area proposed as wash B.Blt. & P. Battalion & read to ascertain water-possibilities in company with A.D.M.S.	
	7		Visited Support Points "MAMIE' salient & west of YPRES - Rode out with D.D.M.S. & D.M.S. Third Army 49th R.F.A. Huts in trenches, 62 and & 59th Corps Engineers, Hospital trenches. I.104.1.74 Gravel.	
			Clearing Station.	
	8		O.C. engaged in inspecting all camps for inspection before proceeding on leave	
	9		O.C. " " " " " " "	
	9		Pte MARSHALL detailed to Capt HAXELL's Subsection in place of Pte MEAD evacuated.	
	10		O.C. started leave	

Army Form C. 2118.

WAR DIARY
or
INTELLIGENCE SUMMARY.
(Erase heading not required.)

Place	Date	Hour	Summary of Events and Information	Remarks and references to Appendices
VLAMERTINGHE	1915 Sept 11		O.C. on leave. Party Sectn. engaged on inspection, as per weekly Report to A.D.M.S.	
	12		" "	
	13		" "	
	14		" "	
	15		" "	
	16		" "	
	17		" engaged on detail work at Hdqtrs.	
	18	MORN	" went to YPRES with DADMS. Visited Ramparts nort of MENIN GATE. Arranged with Sanitary Squad to disinfect house turned sanitary section Building in Rue THOROUT, YPRES	
	19	MORN	Inspected 7th R.B. Camp & Stables in company with A.D.M.S.	
		AFTN	Visited 17th Casualty Clearing Station also No 16 Clearing Station with samples water from Dickebush Farms. Saw O.C. No 1 Mobile Laboratory with reference to examination park. elimin from dickebush card.	
	20		Arranged to bi-weekly testing Water Sources examined water from Storeshoe Farm H.14 & sheet 28 Gave permission to 47th R.F.A. to water horses at pond. Requested A.D. about VMO. 49th R.F.A. to remove horses permanent from pond of Ypres	

1577 Wt. W10791/1773 500,000 1/15 D. D. & L. A.D.S.S./Forms/C. 2118.

Army Form C. 2118.

WAR DIARY
or
INTELLIGENCE SUMMARY.
(Erase heading not required.)

Instructions regarding War Diaries and Intelligence Summaries are contained in F. S. Regs., Part II. and the Staff Manual respectively. Title pages will be prepared in manuscript.

Place	Date	Hour	Summary of Events and Information	Remarks and references to Appendices
VLAMERTINGHE	Sep 21		Inspected the following Camps in Company with D.D.M.S. & A.D.M.S. 8th K.R.R. & 9th K.R.B. 4th K.R.R. in Rear Area & 4th K.R.F.A. in Forward Area	
	22		Revisited Hutments in Reserve Area & arranged for completion of work in line to recuperation on report. 9/23rd and A.D.M. Report work	
	23		Visited YPRES with Sergt. HAXELL & Selected quarters to be cleared out for the accommodation of Stretcher bearers. Visited 42nd Bde Heights & arranged for the immediate employment of 50 men of the Division in cleaning up ramparts north of Menin Gate. Visited Transport Camp of 10th Durham R.I. who are to occupy hutments in area & arranged for the Supply of Latrine Buckets & Rubbish & Sanitary details in connection with Hutments.	
	24		R. Rehman & Hutments altogether of found every thing in readiness for occupation. Engaged in office work	
	25		OC Spent day in A.D.M.S. office dealing with matters thus during of the ADMS & the D.A.D.M.S.	
	26		OC. Visited Advanced Helghu YPRES & arranged for latrine accommodation of officers & men in occupation of N.C.O. in charge of fatigue to Buls Sonne.	
	27		Revisited XIV DIV Baths POPERINGHE & enquire into working of field baths dealing with	

1577 Wt.W10791/1773 500,000 1/15 D.D. & L. A.D.S.S./Forms/C. 2118.

Army Form C. 2118.

WAR DIARY
or
INTELLIGENCE SUMMARY.
(Erase heading not required.)

Instructions regarding War Diaries and Intelligence Summaries are contained in F. S. Regs., Part II. and the Staff Manual respectively. Title pages will be prepared in manuscript.

Place	Date	Hour	Summary of Events and Information	Remarks and references to Appendices
VLAMERTINGHE	Sep 27	pp.m.	Ablution tanks and to the damage done to Theat Disinfectors which is undergoing repair at F.A.W.D. In consultation with M.O. 7th J.R. Bde re treatment of water and washing of scale carts etc. Also demonstrated to A.D.M.S. impurities in chemicals supplied with the Porous cases.	
	28		Tested chemicals impurities found them to be not chemically pure.	
	30		Went to Corpe Hagrs with A.D.M.S. discussed the point of impurity in chemicals	

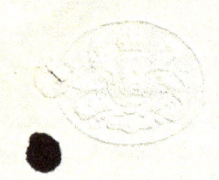

Confidential

War Diary

of

25th Sanitary Section

From 1st October 1915   To 31st October 1915
Volume X 6

E Brooke Pike
Capt.
R.A.M.C.T.
oc
25th Sanitary Section

Army Form C. 2118.

WAR DIARY
or
INTELLIGENCE SUMMARY.
(Erase heading not required.)

Instructions regarding War Diaries and Intelligence Summaries are contained in F. S. Regs., Part II. and the Staff Manual respectively. Title pages will be prepared in manuscript.

Place	Date	Hour	Summary of Events and Information	Remarks and references to Appendices
VLAMERTINGHE	1		Re secret to Army Hdqtrs and A.D.M.S.	
	2		to POPERINGHE re billeting	
			to POPERINGHE re billeting, also to 47th R.F.A. Rendezvous arrangements	
	4		Took section on to POPERINGHE to prepare billets. Sanitary arrangements for Hdqrs.	
	5		to POPERINGHE re billeting	
	6		to 3 Field Ambces to/with D.D.M.S. + A.D.M.S. Visited 49th R.F.A. Relieved Sergt. Bailey to YPRES to supervise construction of sanitary apparatus to 41st Bde Hdqrs Signals. Visited 48th B.A.C. Found Redgerows in an insanitary condition. Told S.M. to put a fatigue to clean it up. Also visited Corps Hdqrs and A.D.M.S. Point Company in afternoon.	
	7		Went to 42nd Bde Hdqrs POPERINGHE re the employing of Corporal. Interviewed Town Major & arranged the matter with him. Visited Baths at POPERINGHE. Received a complaint about the insanitary conditions around Refilling Point. Inspected same & sent in recommendations.	
	8		Inspected premises in YPRES - POPERINGHE Road No77 in connection with a case of Typhoid fever. examined water supply, took same out of Bounds for Troops. Also examined site for new Huts together with Engineer &c.	
	9		Visited Huts & sites to select positions for Latrines etc near BRANDHOEK. Also visited 7th K.R.R. Transports and 8th K.R.R. Transports.	
	10			

A.D.S.S./Forms/C. 2118.

Army Form C. 2118.

WAR DIARY
or
INTELLIGENCE SUMMARY.
(Erase heading not required.)

Instructions regarding War Diaries and Intelligence Summaries are contained in F. S. Regs., Part II. and the Staff Manual respectively. Title pages will be prepared in manuscript.

Place	Date	Hour	Summary of Events and Information	Remarks and references to Appendices
VLAMERTINGHE	1915 Oct 11		O.C. in camp with A.A.&Q.M.G. D.A.D.M.S. & Engineer rearranged tent sites and latrines & arranged for Afflictions Benches.	
	12		Inspected Camp in H12 reoccupied by Shropshires enquired of O.C. steps to put on a telegraphy & clean up field behind Ridge alongside Camp. Visited 42nd Bde Transports (Batt) at H.19. Visit to R.E. & Surveyor of pipe for sanitary work on new Field Dispenser camps occupied by 7 Shropshires & Royal Welch Fusiliers in H.12. The latter had not cleaned up behind the help as requested. Two O.C.'s M10 round to see conditions. Advised general sanitary arrangements of Camp. Received visit from M.O. Royal Welch Fusiliers at Hooge Exhibition wished the unqual Sanitation well. him.	
	13		Visited New Nuthurst with A.A.&Q.M.G. — Reinspected camps P.7 WR stops & Royal Welch Fusiliers. Received order card from 464 R.F.A. B.A.C. falling at unauthorised well, reported same to A.D.M.S.	
	14		Reinlaid with hits to H.1 & P.E. with O.C. 7 4 K.R.R.	
	15		Inspected Huntments in wood at	
	16		Inspected A & B Wards at H.10 & B.8 with A.D.M.S. D.D.M.S. A.A.&Q.M.G. & Capt Frazer R.E. Setting Sanitary arrangements.	

Army Form C. 2118.

WAR DIARY
or
INTELLIGENCE SUMMARY.
(Erase heading not required.)

25 January Section

Instructions regarding War Diaries and Intelligence Summaries are contained in F. S. Regs., Part II. and the Staff Manual respectively. Title pages will be prepared in manuscript.

Place	Date	Hour	Summary of Events and Information	Remarks and references to Appendices
VLAMERTINGHE	1915 Oct 17		Inspected 72nd Bde Transport Camp with Divisional Transport Officer arranged with 2.17 Bde for latrines & Ablution benches. Inspected sites in wood. Saw Matron of Vol. P. & with ADMS	
	18		Inspected 8th KRR and arranged with 2.17. improvements to latrines	
	19		Inspected progress at New Huts trench, including latrines etc. Visited No 17 Barracks. Cleaning Station with A.D.M.S. Inspected Chlorine Spilers at work there. Saw 2 Lt Evans promoted to Lance Corporal and went about pay. Visited C.R.A. with reference to sanitary condition of camp. Visited R.E. Camps & Kings Liverpool Transport Camp. Had same put in order for erect of Corps Bouravarden?	
	20		3.30 p.m. Visit of Corps Commander to exhibition of models of Sanitary appliances at Hdqrs. Return of Surg. Havelle Instructor to 43rd Inf Bde. Saw 2 M. & L. R.R.'s with reference to building of Mildly Room. - Visited B. Hd.qrs. Saw 2 M. & L. R.R. with reference to obtain of Latrine Buckets. Visited part of 41st new Transport camp with Transport Officer & arranged sites for latrines. Ablution Benches etc - lorry sent to CAESTRE for spare pans	
	22		Completed Sites at 41st Base Transports. Visited A Hut 49th Bde R.F.A. with A.D.M.S	
	23		Rode round to 48th Bde R.F.A. & 1st D.A.C. (Advance Sec) arranged sites for latrines	
	24		Visited Base Hospital with A.D.M.S.	

Army Form C. 2118.

WAR DIARY
or
INTELLIGENCE SUMMARY.
(Erase heading not required.)

Instructions regarding War Diaries and Intelligence Summaries are contained in F. S. Regs., Part II. and the Staff Manual respectively. Title pages will be prepared in manuscript.

Place	Date	Hour	Summary of Events and Information	Remarks and references to Appendices
VLAMERTINGHE	1915 Oct 26th		O.C. in all day engaged on weekly Reports &c.	
	26th		Inspected Camps of 6th Somerset R.E. in Rest Area.	
	27th		Interview with O.C. 41st Bde Transport with reference to insanitary condition of 41st Bde Transport Horse Lines	
	28th		Inspected 41st Bde Transport Horse lines and arranged sanitary details	
	29th		Visited Hutments in Wood at H1a Sheet 28 and arranged with 2 M. for disposal of faeces at "B" Huts. Arranged for occupation of B2 Hut by men in tents near wood at H1a	
	30th		O.C. visited Divisional Club POPERINGHE arranged sanitary details. Visited Baths re Chlorination of water. Visited Green Envelope for sanitary fatigue for chit & inspected working of	
	31st		Faeces incinerators at "B" Huts. Engaged all day on reports &c.	

S/

Nov. 1915

14th Blenheim

25th Jan & Feb:
Vol: 7

121/7708

Summarised but not copied

Nov 15.

Confidential

War Diary.

of

25th Sanitary Section.

From 1st November to 30th November, 1915.
(VOL. I.)

E. Woolley Dike
Capt.
O.C.
25th Sanitary Section.

Army Form C. 2118.

WAR DIARY
or
INTELLIGENCE SUMMARY.
(Erase heading not required.)

25th Sanitary Section

Place	Date	Hour	Summary of Events and Information	Remarks and references to Appendices
VLAMERTINGHE	1915 Nov. 1		O.C. engaged on office work, collecting reports from Sub Sections. Section engaged building Orderly Room, laying brick paths etc. O.C. visited 'B' Hut. 3 Sub Sections still attached to the 3 Infantry Brigades for camp inspections.	
	2		O.C. visited 61st R.E. & arranged for latrine seats to be made for Divisional Club POPERINGHE. Also visited POPERINGHE & arranged with ORDNANCE for latrine buckets for the club. Saw Town Major re pickup cart. Visited 29th Bde R.F.A. & 'B' Huts near hutments south of BRANDHOEK.	
	3		O.C. inspected lines vacated by hutments of 3rd Division occupying XIV Division ground. Inspected hutments at BRANDHOEK. Made useful representations to A.A. & Q.M.G. on condition of ground between Rly & the hutments which outside need brick paths. Visited POPERINGHE saw Town Major re pickup cart for our Club.	
	4		Arranged with R.E. for surplus sawdust. Requested Adjutant R.E.s to make enquiries concerning the second storage section with a views to sending it to the Rest Area.	
	5	aft.	Visited Town's Rubbish in wood of H.1.a.5. Saw Q.M. 7th K.R.R. with reference to handling own camp equipment to man to at 'B' Huts. Arranged for brick paths about Heights camp. Paid Section. Visited Boot Club at POPERINGHE. Inspected 29th Bde F.A. Hosp re ABCD Corps.	
	6	aft.	O.C. visited 42nd F.A. & 17th Casualty Clearing Stn with A.D.M.S & D.A.D.M.S.	
			O.C. went to 'D' permanent camp in Rest Area at L.3.a.4.5 & arranged ride for Hosp. all Beathmeet	

WAR DIARY
or
INTELLIGENCE SUMMARY

Army Form C. 2118.

Place	Date	Hour	Summary of Events and Information	Remarks and references to Appendices
VLAMERTINGHE	1915 Nov 6		to use of "C" & "D" Camps. Report writing in afternoon.	
	7	Aft'noon	Interviewed Adjutant of R.E.'s with reference to bar pails & Horsfall incinerators for local incinerators. Inspected Camp of West Riding Division 49 & area vacated by 2nd R.B. Slept by them in an insanitary condition. Reported to same Recommended that a fatigue from unit concerned be sent back to clean up. Brew Horsfall leadnumber from R.E. (incomplete)	
	8		O.C. inspected surroundings of huts & cottages at BRANDHOEK & attached note to Rubbish Dump. Sent Belgian Liaison Officer Vigneulen him to undertook Cottagers & remove some horse refuse to Dump. Went to R.E. for lorries & tools for movement. Received complaint that he walked IN DEN OUID BRANDER was being followed by manure dumped by soldiers. Inspected surroundings manure & heap of clay — well not affected in any way by presence of trooper.	
	9	Aft'n	O.C. went to HOUTKERQUE with A.D.M.S. to inspect Shropshires Camp	
			O.C. inspected huts at BRANDHOEK stopped a field opp Hay hut @ H7c. left turnip field & drill by police 10th Camp Commandant over to see conditions & Saw Officer i/c Bombing class with reference to sanitation of their new camp by 2 J B Huts. Saw P.M.O. 49th Div. H.Q. with reference to employer of labour in hospital	
	10		Sanitary Corps to YPRES % Sergt PEPPER for truck. Took Belgian Liaison Officer round cottages at BRANDHOEK	

Army Form C. 2118.

WAR DIARY
or
INTELLIGENCE SUMMARY.
(Erase heading not required.)

5th Sanitary Section

Place	Date	Hour	Summary of Events and Information	Remarks and references to Appendices
VLAMERTINGHE	1915 Nov 10		training/lecture against insanitary conditions surrounding the cottages	
	11		O.C. visited 41st Bde. H.Q.rs. Transport & Signal Coy R.E. and huts at BRANDHOEK. Recovering	
	12		To PROVEN with A.D.M.S. visited 16th Bde. Inspected continued incinerators, boilers etc.	
	13		O.C. to POPERINGHE – Divisional Baths &c. &c. enquiry	
	14		O.C. weekly report. Inspected 11th Liverpool Regt. Transport also Huts in wood as H.Qrs S/O, out with D.A.D.M.S. Major HEATH returned to 43rd Rota Sub Section. Pte CHECKLEY ret 2 Heights	
	15		KARRIER Lorry broke down in WATON Road	
	16		O.C. visited Bearer Division at RIKKERSBERG CASTLE with A.D.M.S. + D.A.D.M.S. also "B" Huts. Lorry returned to Heights	
	17		Lorry sent to CAESTRE for spring to be repaired. O.C. visited BRANDHOEK "A" + "B" Camps. Also more sanitary arrangements for new church Army Hut	
	18		O.C. saw R.Engineers with reference to down covers for faeces incinerators. Inspected Transport Camps 7th K.R.R., 8th R.B., Somersets, Durhams. Inspected 41st Bde.Heights where part of Section is building Grease Trap, Aldershot Filters & Incinerator.	
	19		O.C. visited Divisional Workshops re accessories for incinerators. Also went to Rest Area with A.D.M.S. +2nd Army O.C. inspected Cyclists Coy Horse Sub Park. O.C. with A.D.M.S. + D.A.D.M.S inspected huts in wood lately occupied	

1577 Wt.W10791/1773 500,000 1/15 D.D.&L. A.D.S.S./Forms/C. 2118.

Army Form C. 2118.

WAR DIARY
or
INTELLIGENCE SUMMARY.
(Erase heading not required.)

Place	Date	Hour	Summary of Events and Information	Remarks and references to Appendices
VLAMERTINGHE	1915 Nov 19		Lorry sent to 100th Coy. A.S.C. DUNKERQUE Rd for coal also to St JAN & BIEZEN.	
	20	Morning	OC worked 42nd R.E. Transport Camp with A.D.M.S. & D.A.D.M.S.	
		Aftn	SC to 6th Corps. R.G. Park to enquire into complaint received from No.1 Sec. D.A.C. as to insanitary conditions obtaining between the R.G. Park and the D.A.C. camp.	
	21		OC saw O/C Hutting and type to move to 7th the trenches etc., OC inspected 11th 4port Transport/ OC went to 6th Corps Park arranged with O.C. R.E. kind for trucking latrine and cleaning up refuse alongside ditch. Weekly Report. Lorry broke down (steering arm broken) arranged to create for repairs	
	22		OC visited BRANDHOEK Park with Camp Commandant to arrange for removal of Atmos dry Hut to Haplrs Pk Ft Kirin examined by D.A.D.M.S. on his application for a Commission. Had Service a British hench shown in map to A.D.M.S. Tested urate from Primary Canal Bank YPRES. Inspected Sub sanitary to doors for incinerator. Railway & working programme for Section for the Register.	
	23		Lorry broke down again – Steering failed – Haw sent to CAESTRE for repair – OC went to HAZEBROCK in search of Roberts & worked arranged for Sanitation for faeces incinerators, OC worked 61st R.E.	
	24		OC went to Transport ROYLI Camp. Arranged for completion of latrine filling in. Also inspected Incinerator incinerary mechanic at BRANDHOEK Hut. Saw 2M Gleaps with refuse to coal for incinerals. w. B. Hut. Inspected latrine in consult of section at Church Army Hut.	

Army Form C. 2118.

WAR DIARY
or
INTELLIGENCE SUMMARY.
(Erase heading not required.)

Place	Date	Hour	Summary of Events and Information	Remarks and references to Appendices
VLAMERTINGHE	1915 Nov 25		O.C. visited Hd.qrs 43rd Bde in Canal Bank YPRES with D.A.A.&Q.M.G. Discussed work of Sanitation with 43rd Bde Staff Major.	
	26		O.C. inspected Transport Camp 42nd Bde.	
	27		O.C. inspected 43rd Bde Transport & L.S. port transport. Arranged with R.E. to whom handed over trenches for A.D.M.S. – Sent 1 two Coal hole incinerators to "B" Knob.	
	28		O.C. engaged in writing Reports.	
	29		O.C. inspected Transport Camp 5th Bn.Brigade in BRANDHOEK Huts. Paris Section arranged.	
	30		O.C. visited 49th R.F.A. & A. Huts.	

25th Jan: Dept.
Vol: 8

131/
7928

/5/

December 1915

F/253/1.

Summarized but not copied

Confidential.

War Diary

of

25th Sanitary Section
R.A.M.C.T.

From 1st December 1915 To 31st December 1915
(Volume) 1.

E Brooke Pike
Capt. O.C.
25th Sanitary Section

WAR DIARY or INTELLIGENCE SUMMARY

Army Form C. 2118.

(Erase heading not required.)

Place	Date	Hour	Summary of Events and Information	Remarks and references to Appendices
VLAMERTINGHE	1915 Dec. 1		O.C. inspected 78th R.F.A., 43rd H. Amble Heights & Church Army Hut.	
	2		O.C. inspected 79th R.F.A. W.P. Huts. Sent Lorry to Amble to ROOSBRUGGE. 3 Cubic echos each conveying 1 F.O.R. attached to the 3 Infantry Brigades for Sanitary inspected.	
	3		1 F.O.R. attached Divl Baths & Theol Disinfector.	
	3		O.C. experimented with Trench Sanitary Heater	
	4		O.C. inspected B Huts & 7 F.P.R. with A.D.M.S.	
	5	Aftn	– attended D.D.M.S.'s Conference at Chateau Couthove. Demonstrated Trench Sanitary Stove. – experimented with flame gas dispersers – also went to 61st Fd/Fd S/B with A.D.M.S.	
	6		– inspected farm at 43rd Bde Hq. Transport in which men are billeted, close site for faeces incinerato at 79th R.F.A. inspected Boil Club Poperinghe – booth No 10 Corwell Canvey Station with A.D.M.S. also demonstrated gas disposal by flame to O.C. & at Helgte –	
	7		O.C. to Poperinghe buying funnels to incinerate Boilers. Inspected Rubawick No 7 F.P.R. WD 5759 KARRIER LORRY sent to 3rd Sanitary Sebn 17th Division and exchanged for DAIMLER Lorry	
	8		W.D. 5857 Driver GEORGE No 073580 and FLETCHER 073578 sent with Karrier Lorry and Driver BEECH No 102634 and MILLICHAP No 102777 attached to this Section in the place	
	9		Sple Chedley No 2432 sent to Army of Amble Post Men to inspect Sanitation of A.B.C&D Standing Camps	

1577 Wt.W10791/1773 500,000 1/15 D.D.&L. A.D.S.S./Forms/C. 2118.

Army Form C. 2118.

WAR DIARY
or
INTELLIGENCE SUMMARY.
(Erase heading not required.)

Place	Date	Hour	Summary of Events and Information	Remarks and references to Appendices
VLAMERTINGHE	1915 Dec.10		O.C. visited HQ 4 R.F.A. to inspect parts unwanted in process of construction; also 62nd Coy R.E. to inspect Machine Gun emplacement & 61st R.E. to arrange for notice boards for trenches for D.A.D.V.S.	
"	11	A/n	To HAZEBROUCK to conduct Boiling to incinerator & chemicals for producing Gas in connection with experiments before the Corps Commander to dispose of gas.	
"	12		Demonstration on Trench Survival Stove & disposing gas by flame before Corps & Divl. Commander. To Divl. Workshops re accessories for same.	
"	13		O.C. engaged in weekly report for A.D.M.S.	
"	14		O.C. proceeded on leave – Pte GILDERSLEVE proceeded on leave.	
"	15	Night	O.C. on leave. Section at Hd Qtrs at work building Traces incinerator & Roofs Cabin inspecting Camps. Lorry sent to HAZEBROUCK to new track tyre.	
"	16		O.C. on leave Sections Hd Qtrs on Traces incinerator etc. Lorry repd.	
"	17		O.C. on leave " " " " " "	
"	18		" " " " " "	
"	19		" " " " " "	
"	20		" " " Smoke helmet inspection by D.A.D.M.S.	

25th Sanitary Section

Army Form C. 2118.

WAR DIARY
or
INTELLIGENCE SUMMARY.
(Erase heading not required.)

Place	Date	Hour	Summary of Events and Information	Remarks and references to Appendices
VLAMERTINGHE	1915 Dec 21		O.C. posted Billeting Certificate for Hqrs Section with Burgomaster. Disposed of Damage claims with farmer at Hqrs - withdrawn. Also inspected 7 KRRC in B Huts & Arrayed with 2/17th Yorks/Wilts Battalion to be burnt in movements at Brandhoek.	
	. 22		O.C. inspected 49th Bn R.F.A.	
	. 23		Demonstrated exhibition of improvised Sanitary appliances at Hqrs, filled in holes etc.	
	. 24		Loaded lorry to departure. Made inventory of Stores taken & left behind. Called at Div Baths & arranged for man % Thread Hy unit. O.C. wrote instructions to Sergt i/c Subsection with reference to travelling with his Brigade to new destination.	
	25		Dispatched lorry to O.C. 19th Div Supply Column with 2 drivers & 1 N.C.O. – Move cancelled	
	26		Lorry returned from Column. O.C. visited 49th R.F.A.; temporary in airport.	
	27		O.C. visited "B" huts BRANDHOEK Church Army Hut. Surroundings of C.R.A. Camp. Wrote to appointment O.C. 19th Divl Sanitary Section to discuss Sanitation before taking on Hqrs Area.	
	28		O.C. in consultation with R.O. 49th Bde R.F.A. & O.S. R.E.	
	29	Morn	Consultation with O.C. Sanitary Section 49th Division. Visited partly new area with him & inspected incinerators etc.	
		Aft	Rode out with D.A.D.M.S. to Hospital Farm, 49th Division Baths etc.	

Army Form C. 2118.

WAR DIARY
or
INTELLIGENCE SUMMARY.
(Erase heading not required.)

Place	Date	Hour	Summary of Events and Information	Remarks and references to Appendices
VLAMERTINGHE	1915 Dec 30		Received work map of new area. Visited Elverdinghe Chateau being vacated by 49 Division. Huts & urinals infected & drained to BRANDHOEK dismantled and re-erected in more suitable spots	
	31	MORN	Gas Helmet inspection (Complete) S.C. visited Divisional Workshop and inspected divisional Club	
		AFTN.	O.C. went to HAZEBRUCK with A.D.M.S. & D.A.D.M.S. & No 12 C.C.S. &c.	

[Stamp: 25th SANITARY SECTION R.A.M.C.]

Elles

Vide D.R.O. 1029.

NOMINAL ROLL

NUMBER	RANK	NAME	CORPS
2149	Staff Sergt.	FULLER. L.S.	R.A.M.C.T.
2392	Sergt.	HAXELL. W.A.B.	"
2397	"	PEPPER. W.	"
2380	"	BAILEY. A.H.	"
2372	Corpl	HEATHER. N.	"
2371	L/Corpl	KIRK. J.A.	"
2395	"	HEATH. J.A.	"
2396	"	HOLLIS. A.	"
2349	"	CLARK. W.T.	"
2432	"	CHECKLEY	"
2367	"	FILKINS. E.W.	"
2350	Private	BISHOP. F.A.	"
2208	"	ALLWRIGHT. H.	"
2676	"	CRULEY. G	"
2427	"	DYER J.W.	"
2388	"	FLINT. C.B.	"
2193	"	GILDERSLEYE H.P.	"
2384	"	HATTON. S.	"
2386	"	JOHNSTONE. T.	"
2366	"	KEITH. W	"
2331	"	McCOY. H	"
2339	"	MARSHALL H T	"
2383	"	MACKAY. D.	"
2387	"	PALMER. W.C	"
2346	"	ROGERS. C.W	"
2277	"	SMITH. H.	"
102634	"	BEECH R. E.	M.T. A.S.C.
102777	"	MILLICHAP. W.E.	"

Officers.

Capt. E Brooke Pike R.A.M.C. (T.F.)

San: Sect: 25
Vol: 9

F/253/2
14

Jan. 1916.

Army Form C. 2118.

WAR DIARY
or
INTELLIGENCE SUMMARY.
(Erase heading not required).

Place	Date	Hour	Summary of Events and Information	Remarks and references to Appendices
VLAMERTINGHE	1916 JAN 1	am	O.C. inspected Red Horse ELVERDINGHE. Heights 48 R.T.A. to map unresiftate conflagration M.O. about bad smell from drain under house. Discussed remaining when word M.O. O.C.	
		Aft.	Attended R.A.M.C. Conference at Corps Hghts	
	2	am	O.C. went to Ag't Divl Area to select sites for central Incinerator	
		aft	Engaged on Reports	
	3		O.C. went to Incinerator at A18C to Divl Workshop to arrange for materials to building new incinerator	
		Aft.	Inspected No's 1 & 2 camps at A16 P & A16 C with A.D.M.S. & D.A.D.M.S.	
	4	am	O.C. inspected Whitepool Transport Camp with A.D.M.S.	
		Aft	Attended Gas Demonstration. Washed Khaki through fumes fumes of Chlorine. Inspected Dump at Incinerator at A18C. Ground work of cleaning up being carried on by a Corpl & 10 men. J. 42 × 79 Indicated on Town Map at POPERINGHE with reference to removal of freecis from Latlets in to from Various Burgomast. VLAMERTINGHE with Billeting certificate	
	5		Inspected ELVERDINGHE Chateau & camps in grounds occupied by Whippers, 9 4KRR & York LI Arranged Sanitary detail work R.O. 11th Kings Lpool. Visited 6 S.W.R.S. Park remanded & supply) Sanitary Section. Engaged building Incinerator at 92nd Bde Transport Camp. Prepared Staff hills for full agreements.	Capt. OC 254 San Sec

EMc

Army Form C. 2118.

WAR DIARY
or
INTELLIGENCE SUMMARY.
(Erase heading not required.)

Place	Date	Hour	Summary of Events and Information	Remarks and references to Appendices
VLAMERTINGHE	1916 JAN 6		Helmet parade with drill. OC inspected ELVERDINGHE Chateau and proceeded with ADMS & ODMS & visited Camps No 3 & 4 with ACMS	
	7		Inspected Camp at A'Hut before coming up by 10 to D.L.I. - Luncheon with OC 6th Gen. Sec. and afterwards making sanitary inspection of outside units in 14th Div Area. Inspected Mch Machine Gun Section at Reynier Farm & Walker Hospital Farm	
	8		OC visited Central Incinerator Dumps. Found fatigue party at work. (42nd F.A.) Obtained fatigue from No 1 Coy 4 Eukenching Battalion for work on the incinerator. Inspected Camp of Eukenching Battalion. Arranged with OC Div Workshops to provide rakes for use at Central Incinerator Dumps.	
	9		OC in office engaged on reports.	
	10		OC inspected work at Central Incinerator Dumps. Also inspected No 1 Corps Farm with A.D.M.S	
	11		OC made water reconnaissance at S'Liste Couvent. Obtained sample water from 3 local sources used by No 4 Camp. Tested vermclennel. Arranged water distribution in new Area. Consultation with AA & 2 MG Reserves in new Area & Sanitation generally. Sgt Potter No 2391 evacuated sick (temporily). Pte Gildersleve No 2193 evacuated sick (permanent).	
	12		Inspected Well at A21 a 6.4 Sheet 28 reported no work required here. Found large supply water available at New spot - Inspected Hdqs to Eukenching Battalion.	

1577 Wt.W10791/1773 500,000 1/15 D.D.&L. A.D.S.S./Forms/C. 2118.

Army Form C. 2118.

WAR DIARY
or
INTELLIGENCE SUMMARY
(Erase heading not required).

Instructions regarding War Diaries and Intelligence Summaries are contained in F. S. Regs., Part II, and the Staff Manual respectively. Title Pages will be prepared in manuscript.

Place	Date	Hour	Summary of Events and Information	Remarks and references to Appendices
VLAMERTINGHE	1916 12	Night	O.C. inspected heap of refuse at Essex Farm left by 49th Div. & also & canal bank in neighbourhood.	
	13		Reported on sanitary condition of Essex Farm neighbourhood. Inspected St Sixte - South Pole. Sent 'rain shelter for latrine site & arranged for Div. Workshops to largely material. Sent Spt J Sechin to fuel incinerator at 43rd Bore Transport Camp.	
	14		Took men to St Sixte then Brick & cement coping put round well in yard. Completed experiments on use of Anthracite Buff fuel in brazier.	
	15		Reported on Anthracite Buff fuel. Inspected M.No6 Hospital work recommended by Colonel Hutchin Shaeft. Spt. Hewitt No.2277 promoted to L/Corpl without extra pay.	
	16		Inspected Central Dump A18C (Sheet 28) & instructed Corp. in charge as to sterilizing sack of sacks left there. Took cover for well to St Sixte. To Rest Stn with A.D.M.S. Weekly report.	
	17		To Brielen re. Water supply & latrine accommodation. Tested 5 waters from New Area.	
	18		To No. 1 & 2 Camps & to St Sixte to arrange billeting & rationing of men sent to reside at camps. Sgts. of Sub-Sections brought to Hd.Qrs — gave instructions as to their duties under new scheme. Sgt. Haxell to No. 4 camp with Pte. Marshall, Sgt. Bailey, Pte. Mackay to No. 3 Camp, L.Corp. Kirk & Pte. Dyer to No. 3 Coy A.S.C., L.Corp. Smith & Pte. Rogers to 'A' huts, L.Corp. Jilkins to Transport Camp with Pte. Johnstone, L.Corp. Hollis to Bde. Billets in Poperinghe, Staff Sgt. Fuller - L.Corp. McCoy & Pte. Allwright to Nos 1 & 2 Camps. (Pte. McCoy No. 2321 promoted to L.Corp. without extra pay). L.Corp. Heath to 'B' Huts.	
	19		Sample of water from 'De Rust Plaats' where men were found filling water bottles was satisfactory. Saw O.C. 29th Field Co RE with reference to arranging pipes	O.C. 254 Sany Sec

Army Form C. 2118.

WAR DIARY
or
INTELLIGENCE SUMMARY
(Erase heading not required).

Instructions regarding War Diaries and Intelligence Summaries are contained in F. S. Regs., Part II, and the Staff Manual respectively. Title Pages will be prepared in manuscript.

Place	Date 1916.	Hour	Summary of Events and Information	Remarks and references to Appendices
VLAMERTINGHE. (continued)	January 19.		4 tanks at well, A21b (Sheet 28).	
	20.		To Trois Tours, Brielen with reference to drainage & emptying cesspit. Reported on same to A.D.M.S.	
	21-26 (inclusive)		Absent on dental sick leave. (Pte. C.B.Flick on leave 24.1.16.)	
	27.		Work in office. Visited well at A21b (Sheet 28). Saw Engineers re progress of work there.	
	28.		Inspected 'A' Huts.	
	29.		Visited Divl. Workshops with reference to material on indent. Visited Steinzje Mill. Visit of D.A.D.M.S. Second Army.	
	30.		To Nos 1 & 2 Camps to select site for Horsfall disinfector being removed from central dump A18c. Obtained permission from A.A.Q.M.G. for occupation & Armstrong Hut by San. Sub Section at these camps & its removal to a more convenient site. Weekly Report to No.17 C.C.S. with A.D.M.S.	
	31.		To R.E. camps with M.O. & C.O. R.E. To No.3 camp with gear for incinerator. To Hazebrouck - ordered kit water tank for incinerator. Lc-Cpl Zilkins 2367 on leave.	

E. Dorothy Litt
Capt.
O.C.
25th San. Sec.

14th Bn.

25th Saus Sectn.

Feb. 1916

Sau: Sect: 25
Vol: 10

Army Form C. 2118.

WAR DIARY
or
INTELLIGENCE SUMMARY

(Erase heading not required).

Place	Date	Hour	Summary of Events and Information	Remarks and references to Appendices
VLAMERTINGHE	1916. February			
	1.		To No. 3 Camp to inspect progress of work on tanks at Droogentak. No. 1 Camp re case of scarlet fever - sent spray to disinfect huts.	
	2.		Wrote to O.C. 4th Labour Batt. asking him to remove burnt tins at central Dump A 18 c. Inspected No.s 3 & 4 camps. Close site at No.4 camp for faeces incinerator. To Divl. Workshops re stores for camps. Plan of incinerators sent to Lc-Cpls Heath, Smith, Kirk & Sgt. Bailey.	
	3.		Inspected "A" Huts. To Hazebrouck with A.D.M.S. - collected tank ordered on 31st ultimo. Pte Keath to No.4 Camp to erect Faeces Destructor. (Plan of same given him.)	
	4.		Inspected progress of work on well at A 21 a. Visited No.s 1 & 4 camps	
	5.		Sent Lc-Cpl. McCoy 2331. on leave (extra vacancy) Instructed Sam. Sec (Sub-sec) No.1 Camp to inspect R.F.A. camps on Wooster Road. Sent plan of Faeces Destructor to Lc-Cpl Clarke 42nd Bde Transport	
	6.		Visited 9th Field Co. R.E. re work at well A 21 a. Visited No. 4 Camp. Visited Divl. Workshops re trench boards & stores. Visited 4th Field Amb. at Divl. Rest Station. Saw O.C. re sanitation of his area.	

BSD - B. M3o1. 22/11. 12/15. 5000.

Army Form C. 2118.

WAR DIARY
or
INTELLIGENCE SUMMARY
(Erase heading not required).

Instructions regarding War Diaries and Intelligence Summaries are contained in F. S. Regs., Part II. and the Staff Manual respectively. Title Pages will be prepared in manuscript.

Place	Date 1916	Hour	Summary of Events and Information	Remarks and references to Appendices
VLAMERTINGHE.	February 7		(Continued.) Visited Nos 3 + 4 Camps. Inspected well at Asra.	
	8		To Divl. Workshops re. drain pipes. Weekly Report. To Hazebrouck with A.D.M.S. - ordered tank for second faeces Incinerator.	
	9		Spent day with O.C. XX Div. Sanitary Section discussing water + sanitation of Divl. Area. Visited various camps + water sources, etc.	
	10		Visited Nos 1, 3, + 4 Camps to arrange for cleaning up before evacuation. To Hazebrouck to collect tank ordered on the 8th inst. To No 3 Camp for Sgt. Bailey + Pte. Mackay. - rejoined 4th Brigade. - also L-Corps Hollis + Smith. Sent men in charge of faeces Incinerator at 'B' Huts to rejoin their units after completion of days work.	
	11		To 43rd Fld. Amb. to arrange for attached men working on Incinerator dump to rejoin their unit. Dispatched Sgt.+Sgt Fuller + Pte Allwright to Warmhoudt to rejoin 4th Brigade. - also L-Corp Filkins. Dispatched Sgt. Hazell, Pte. Marshall, L-Corp Heath + L-Corp Clark to Hawkesque to rejoin 3rd Brigade.	
	12		Dispatched lorry + guard to Esquelbecq with Sanitary Section gear. Remainder of Section moved into new billets at Esquelbecq.	
ESQUELBECQ.	13			

BSD - B. M351.22/11. 12/15. 500J.

Army Form C. 2118.

WAR DIARY
or
INTELLIGENCE SUMMARY

(Erase heading not required).

Instructions regarding War Diaries and Intelligence Summaries are contained in F. S. Regs., Part II, and the Staff Manual respectively. Title Pages will be prepared in manuscript.

Place	Date 1916	Hour	Summary of Events and Information	Remarks and references to Appendices
ESQUELBECQ.	February 14.		Arranged latrine accommodation at Odosanne, Signal R.E's, Cyclists etc. Dug trench latrines at West end & middle of town. Saw Mayor with reference to water supply. Rode to Zuggers Cappel to enquire into reported case of scarlet fever. Interviewed Major + Med. Officer - found no trace of such a case in the town.	
	15.		Arranged for repairs to pump in Square by F.A.W.U. Tested water at Estaminet "Nouvelle de la Forge (used by Ad.Q's cooks), also sample from 4th Div! Signal Transport - Ash waters required ½ scoop Bleaching Powder per 100 galls. Arranged for Officer's latrine in Chateau grounds. Inspected sanitary arrangements of Cyclist Coy + M.M.G. Section camps. Go to 43rd, 44th Field Ambs. with A.D.M.S. Pte. Keith No 2366 on leave.	
	16.		Rode to Zuggers-Cappel - Interviewed Major + Medical Officer with reference to case of scarlet fever, reported by XX Division. Both denied existence of such a case which would have been reported to them if it had occurred. To St. Omer with A.D.M.S.	
	17.		Having ascertained location of reported case of Scarlet fever, rode to Zuggers-Cappel & found such a case had occurred at "Debit des Boissons" (Next door to "Estaminet à la Ville de Cassel") - an Officer having been ill for two days. The 2 rooms he occupied had afterwards been disinfected & were occupied by another officer who left 14 days ago. — No further steps taken.	

BSD - B. M351.22/41. 12/15 5000f.

Army Form C. 2118.

WAR DIARY
or
INTELLIGENCE SUMMARY
(Erase heading not required).

Place	Date 1916.	Hour	Summary of Events and Information	Remarks and references to Appendices
ESQUELBECQ.	February 17	(continued)	Visited Field Cashier at Wormhoudt & paid men.	
			Tested Village pump water, after pumping one hour (Result: Water required 2 scoops Bleach Powder.) Two hours later it required 3 scoops Bleach Powder — had pump closed for 24 hrs.	
	18.		Again tested pump water (Result: 4 scoops Bleach Powder) — pump again closed for 24 hrs.	
			Sent lorry to Arneke Station to collect & distribute Officers' men returned from leave.	
			Lc Col Kirk No 257, applying for Commission, was medically examined by D.A.D.M.S. & his application forwarded to the War Office, London.	
FLESSELLES.	19.		Moved to FLESSELLES with A.D.M.S.	
	20.		Unit moved to FLESSELLES with Ad.Qrs.	
			Officer made reconnaissance of village with reference to water & sanitation.	
			Unit arrived FLESSELLES & took up billets.	
	21.		Lorry left ESQUELBECQ with M.A.W.U.	
	22.		Unit engaged on sanitary duties.	
			Lorry arrived from ESQUELBECQ.	
	23.		Water tested at pumps & wells — supplies labelled.	
			Plan for latrines etc. prepared & sent to Engineers.	

WAR DIARY
or
INTELLIGENCE SUMMARY

(Erase heading not required.)

Army Form C. 2118.

Place	Date	Hour	Summary of Events and Information	Remarks and references to Appendices
	1916 February			
DOULLENS.	24.		Unit moved with Ad. Qrs to DOULLENS.	
SUS. ST. LEGER.	25.		Unit moved with Ad. Qrs to SUS. ST. LEGER. Hard frost & heavy snowstorms - transport delayed on roads & did not arrive till next day.	
	26. 27. 28.		Unit on Sanitary duty in the Village.	
BARLY.	29.		Left SUS ST. LEGER & arrived at BARLY. Tested Village water supplies & arranged latrine accomodation.	

Moore?
Capt
O.C.
26th San. Sec.

14th Divn

25 dan See
Vol II

March 1916

Army Form C. 2118.

WAR DIARY
or
INTELLIGENCE SUMMARY.
(Erase heading not required.)

Instructions regarding War Diaries and Intelligence Summaries are contained in F. S. Regs., Part II. and the Staff Manual respectively. Title pages will be prepared in manuscript.

25th SANITARY SECTION No. ...

Place	Date	Hour	Summary of Events and Information	Remarks and references to Appendices
Pally Bonneville	1916 April 1st		Unit engaged on sanitary work.	
	2nd		Left Pally, arrived Bonneville. Work was immediately started on water reconnaissance, and sanitary enquiries. Water found to be very good and sanitation non-existant. Basin cleaned out and water and disinfected for use of "D" officers and signals.	
	3rd		Officer visited Arras on water reconnaissance. 1st & 2nd Officers steps cleaned out and disinfected. Water reconnaissance and test made of sources at Linencourt — and wells labeled. Unit engaged on sanitary work generally. Sent lorry to railhead to collect 100 latrine buckets for use of village.	
	4th		Reported to A.D.M.S. on sanitation of Bonneville with plans etc reported also on water supply of Arras. Unit engaged on constructional work.	
	5th		Visited Linencourt. Inspected water supply. Saw Staff Captain of 12th Lf Div.	
	6th		Visited Domville with A.D.M.S. and D.A.D.&L. To Doallens to purchase stores.	

1577 Wt.W10791/1773 500,000 1/15 D.D.&L. A.D.S.S./Forms/C. 2118.

WAR DIARY or INTELLIGENCE SUMMARY

Army Form C. 2118.

Place	Date	Hour	Summary of Events and Information	Remarks and references to Appendices
Bonneville	1916 April 1st		Sent report on Arras water supply to A.D.M.S. — Visited afresh same morning. Saw Chef des Compagnies des Eaux. Eight fatigue arrived, arranged billeting etc.	
		8	Visited Arras with reference to sanitation. Saw Town Major. Arranged labour bucket distribution with D.A.Q.M.G. Plan of Arras to A.D.M.S. with report on sanitation. Report on sanitation of Bonneville to A.D.M.S.	
		9	Arranged with R.E.'s re Corporal re building of latrines. Report on proposed sanitation of Demicourt to A.D.M.S. (Copy of do.) — Stade arrangement for motor pumps.	
		10	Sent Corporal Kirk, 1st Batt. Falkirks, Ptes Dyer & Rogers to Town Major Lowers. Town Major of Lowers to look after sanitation. Barbs & severs. Wrote to A.D.M.S. re Refuse destructors for the five villages in Dist. area. Re Type and Sawhall (two reinforcements reported. Lorry to workshops for repairs.	
		11:15	Report and plan of proposed baths combined with refuse incinerator sent to Col. Howell	

Army Form C. 2118.

WAR DIARY
or
INTELLIGENCE SUMMARY.
(Erase heading not required.)

Place	Date	Hour	Summary of Events and Information	Remarks and references to Appendices
Doullens	Nov 11th		Lce Cpl. Clark, Pte Hatton & Pte Marshall to Arras to be attached to S.M.O., Arras. Wrote to D.A.Q.M.G. re fatigue of eight men for Humencourt. Sent from Major Dept of mobile vetn in Berneville.	
	12th		Plan of Arras to A.A.D.M.S.	
	13th		Plan of fresh districts to Lt. D. Arras. Inspected sanitation at Doullens. Sprayed huts at Corbelle-Wezin (6th South D.) Officer to R.E. Park Doullens. Visited 5th Divl. Sanitary Officer at Banquetin, and arranged for latrines and buckets to be taken over with billets in Barquetin.	
	14th		Wrote to A.D.M.S. re permanent fatigues at Doullens, Lucheux, Warluc and Barquetin. Also fatigues of four men and one at O. to deal with horse manure at Berneville, Lucheux and Humencourt. Wrote to A.D.M.S. re general latrine & urinal system trade arrangements re rationing and billeting of the 68 cobby & Pte Rogers (returned from Pollens) left in Berneville. Asking Cpl. d'Heatle to be left with part of Corporal. Today to Arras at night to relieve clothes from	Ellis

Army Form C. 2118.

WAR DIARY
or
INTELLIGENCE SUMMARY
(Erase heading not required.)

Instructions regarding War Diaries and Intelligence Summaries are contained in F.S. Regs., Part IV. and the Staff Manual respectively. Title Pages will be prepared in manuscript.

Place	Date	Hour	Summary of Events and Information	Remarks and references to Appendices
Bernaville	March 16		Officers to Barlus re billets and latrines. See Cpl. Heap to see if without extra help. To Bielle Mon to be attached to 6th Corps H.Q. shaped out huts at Bielle Mon, shade map of Hauteville. C.O. to Arras to inspect sanitary condition of St. Sauveur – settled with G.O.C. on method of cleaning up and fatigues necessary.	
Barlus	" 17		Moved to Barlus. Made arrangements for latrines for "C" and "D" officers and A.D.M.S. Began survey of water source of village, billets with R.E. officers on nights in Barlus, Dangoein, Hauteville and Follures for public latrines. Inspected proposed Dis. school at Hauteville with O.C. and made arrangements for fatigue for cleaning up. Silbert to clean up and repair Lee hut.	
	" 18		See Cpl. Gilbert and Cpl. Eyre to Hauteville to look after sanitation. Made arrangements to Barlus and billet arrangements for Warluns.	
	" 19		To R.E. park with reference to stoles. To Dangoein with light cart to see sanitary billets which were offered to the A.D. of L. bo pamined cart and and reported verbally to A.D. of L.	
	20		To 62nd R.E.'s at Danville, to stoves and of then wire to Wellin O wells etc. to Dangoein. Saw Town major with reference to sanitary cart.	(Ellis)

2449 Wt. W14957/Mgo 750,000 1/16 J.B.C. & A. Forms/C.2118/12.

Army Form C. 2118.

WAR DIARY
or
INTELLIGENCE SUMMARY

(Erase heading not required.)

Instructions regarding War Diaries and Intelligence Summaries are contained in F. S. Regs., Part II. and the Staff Manual respectively. Title Pages will be prepared in manuscript.

Place	Date	Hour	Summary of Events and Information	Remarks and references to Appendices
Dahus	Mch 20th 1916		of town, also taking and billeting of Sub Sector. He inconvt to select sight for disposal of to be manure to Sanguin will A.D.S.1 & 42nd Field Ambulance — Visited O.A.D.M.	
	21st		Ice Cpl Smith and Pte Hatton to Havebrucke. Pte Cpl Zilkins & Pte Eyre to Sanguin. Had orders published re D.R.O. with reference to treatment of site manure. Selected sight for disposal of horse manure at Bouille. Saw O.C. of No 1 Mobile Lab with reference to extermination of Liverpool Varmus for destruction of rats. Requested signals to that up lights in field behind office Dis yard and to remove latrine unsuitable to another site.	
	22nd		to Regts and Army H.Qs — Royals and 8th Bat with A.D.M.S.1	
	23rd		to Renieville and divisions re disposal of manure etc, took manure forks and watering cart for use in their village. Inspected affaire of Dashes re P. Niggin of Refuse pits in fields required for cultivation of corps. — Arranged another site Lce Cpl Follis to special duty being Pte Haines and deal (reinforcements) reported. Saw claire of Wasken in chg of Millege Sick general inspection of sanitation of millege	

2449 Wt. W14957/M90 750,000 1/16 J.B.C. & A. Forms/C.2118/12.

WAR DIARY or INTELLIGENCE SUMMARY

Army Form C. 2118.

Place	Date	Hour	Summary of Events and Information	Remarks and references to Appendices
Bailleul	Feb 25		To Hinderville to arrange site for manure dump with R.E. Despatched Pte. Ebal to Doulieu to pitcase the Opl. Hosp. stile on leave. Took Cpl. Hearne to Borre H. Qrs. to obtain details of maps of bath area obtained by D.D.M.S. Bought buckets for use at wells in Bailleul.	
	26		Engaged all day on reports of sanitation of Division.	
	27		At Bailleul on inspections and arranged site for manure dump to Handcourt (142nd Bde. H.Q.) with regard to water reconnaissance at Agny. To Arras to 2/2 Field Ambulance (new beds showering Mn)	
	28		To Bouzeville and Hendecourt re sites for Hospitals destricts To Sanguelin re mvy of village. To Hackerville to settle with C.O.C.O. sites for Hospital closenclos.	
	29		To Hébuterne (144 Field Ambulance) and to Souastre to check maps. In afternoon to Doullens to see S.S.O.	
	30			
	31		Visited R.E. Park + C.R.E. in connection with building public latrines in the various villages. To Lauroy to see Sanitary officer 56th Division in view of possible change over.	Brooke Ryles Capt. C. R. & S.(?)

WAR DIARY

of

25th Sanitary Section

for

April 1916

Army Form C. 2118.

25 San Sec
vol 12

WAR DIARY
or
INTELLIGENCE SUMMARY

(Erase heading not required.)

Place	Date	Hour	Summary of Events and Information	Remarks and references to Appendices
WARLUS	1916 April 1st		Completed plans & reports of sanitation schemes of the villages of the Divl. Area & sent same to A.D.Med. Services for action. Arranged for the distribution of latrine baskets (?) at Arras.	
	2nd		Office work all day settling up plans etc. Wrote to A.D.Med. Services, G.M.Os of the various villages & NCOs I/c Sub-Sections with regard to treatment of manure.	
	3rd–4th		On leave. 2nd April – sent I/c detail drawing of ablution bench to G.M.O. Hauteville.	
			L/c HOLLIS returned from leave	
			8th April – L/c HOLLIS to FOSSEUX.	
			12th April – Supplementary sanitation scheme of FOSSEUX to C.R.E. for execution.	
	5th		Made arrangements for lecture on Sanitation at Divl. Schools, Hauteville. To Berneville & Simencourt on general inspection.	
	6th		L/c HOLLIS returned to DAINVILLE. Pte CLEAL to FOSSEUX. Made arrangements to build brick incinerator at Divl. Schools Hauteville. Plan of draining pit for forgful Destructor to G.M.O. Berneville.	
	7th		To Wanquetin on general inspection. Sanitary models being prepared for lectures at Divl. Schools, Hauteville.	

2449 Wt. W14957/M90 750,000 1/16 J.B.C. & A. Forms/C.2118/12.

Army Form C. 2118.

WAR DIARY
or
INTELLIGENCE SUMMARY
(Erase heading not required.)

Place	Date	Hour	Summary of Events and Information	Remarks and references to Appendices
WARLUS	April (continued) 17th (cont.)		To Hauteville - saw O.C. Div Schools - made arrangements + chose sites for he various models. Chose sites for ablution benches for Div. Hd. Qrs in Chateau grounds. Prepared plans of proposed latrine for O.C. 50 Seige Battery, R.G.A. (near Mallus) to O.C., R.E. Park, to arrange for materials.	
	18th		To Dainville on general inspection.	
	19th		Visited D.D.N.S, 6th Corps, at Noyelle Vion - made arrangements for permanent latrines at 16 Flying Squadron camp. To Fosseux on general inspection.	
	20th		Drew brushes for incinerator at School of Instruction, Hauteville. Wrote to C.R.E. requesting him to erect tanks for chlorination of water in AGNY. To S.R.O. to attend a lecture on gas at 3rd Army Hd.qrs.	
	21st		To Hauteville, Div. Schools re sanitary work in hand here. To Avesnes-le-Comte + Noyelle Vion - called on D.D.M.S - arranged with Sgt. HEATH to make a model of a standard latrine for lecturing purposes. Took plan of latrine to Flying Squadron camp + arranged for its erection. To S.S.O. re cocks for filter beds at School of Instruction, Hauteville.	
	22nd		To Hauteville Div. Schools on general inspection. To Gt. Corps H.Qrs. W.A.D.M.S. to attend conference.	

Army Form C. 2118.

WAR DIARY
or
INTELLIGENCE SUMMARY
(Erase heading not required.)

Instructions regarding War Diaries and Intelligence Summaries are contained in F.S. Regs., Part II. and the Staff Manual respectively. Title Pages will be prepared in manuscript.

25th Sanitary Section

Place	Date	Hour	Summary of Events and Information	Remarks and references to Appendices
WARLUS.	April (continued)			
	23rd		To Hauteville re Sanitary work here - models completed. Visited 2 Field Ambulance at Dainguekin - inspected horse manure disposal ground.	
	24th		To Gouyeux on general inspection. Prepared notes for lecture at Div. Schools Hauteville. At Malus in afternoon on general inspection.	
	25th		Visited villages of 56th Div. Area (Rest) with A.P.M. Lecture on sanitation at Div. Schools.	
	26th		Erection of brick incinerator + climb at Hauteville Div. Schools in hand. Visited Berneville - saw Q.M.O. + Town Major. Visited Simencourt - inspected dumping ground + incinerator. To Gouyeux - to 26th Mobile Vet. Section + Div. Schools, Hauteville, on general inspection.	
	27th		To Royalle - now to see Sgt. HEATH int reference to models. To Hauteville on general inspection. Section continued work at Div. Schools.	
	28th		To Dainville re treatment of manure + use of disinfectants. Sent to 6th Corp Adjors with reference to models. To Avesnes-le-Comte + Hauteville re sanitary work in hand.	

Army Form C. 2118.

WAR DIARY
or
INTELLIGENCE SUMMARY

(Erase heading not required.)

Place	Date	Hour	Summary of Events and Information	Remarks and references to Appendices
WARLUS.	1916 April (continued).			
	28th (cont.)		Sent ½ FILKINS' application for a commission in a Sanitary Coy to Territorial Force Association.	
			To Wanquetin re Horse manure.	
			Sanitary models at School of Instruction completed.	
	29th		To Wanquetin to see G.M.O.	
			Saw O.C. 2nd Fld. Amb re Faeces Incinerator.	
			Reconnaissance for wells suitable for erection of pumps + tanks by 3rd Army Engineer.	
	30th		To Dainville to see G.M.O.	
			To O.C. R.E. Park re indents for materials.	
			To Gt. Corps Hdqrs. re models of sanitary appliances.	

E. Brookfield
Capt.
O.C.
25th San. Sec.

"25 Sar S/c.
Vol 13

Confidential

War Diary

of

25th Sanitary Section
R.A.M.C. (T.F.)

From 1st May 1916   To 31st May 1916

Capt
OC
25th Sanitary Section

COMMITTEE FOR THE
MEDICAL HISTORY OF THE WAR
Date 26 JUN 1915

WAR DIARY
or
INTELLIGENCE SUMMARY
(Erase heading not required).

Army Form C. 2118.

Place	Date	Hour	Summary of Events and Information	Remarks and references to Appendices
MARLUS.	1916 May 1st		To Mangueton + Fosseux on general sanitary inspection.	
	2nd		Sent plans of latrines (SM 7 & 8) to Sergt. Heath to make models of same. L/C McCoy to hospital, sick. L/C McCoy 2331 evacuated to hospital, sick. To Fosseux re erection of latrines + incinerator at Fld. Amb. Camp. Writing up sanitary notes. Section laid experimental floor for latrines of petrol tins cut in half + filled with chalk + inverted (jointed in cement).	
	3rd		To Boulogne with DDMS + DADMS to inspect sanitary arrangements of Rest Camp. Sent L/Cpl. Hollis to replace L/Cpl. McCoy - sick. Sent full size working drawings of Sharpes Urine trough to CRE for execution. To Noyelle-Vion to see Sergt. Heath re models. To Manqueton to see Major Smeeth re erection of (screen, incinerator, etc.)	
	4th		To Hauteville to Divl. Schools.	
	5th		Saw OC XxQ Noble Lab. with regard to water sources in Divl. Area. To Manqueton to inspect wet which was being cleaned out - called for 2nd Fld. Amb. S/Sgt. Tiller, Ptes. Allwright + Marshall evacuated Simencourt + took over Berneville. L/Cpl. Hollis returned to Dainville. Capt. Kirk, Ptes. Dyer + Cleal evacuated Fosseux + returned to HdQrs.	
	6th		Inspected well at Manqueton in process of cleaning - also 3 other wells with a view to one having tanks & pumps erected for filling water carts.	

WAR DIARY or INTELLIGENCE SUMMARY

Place	Date	Hour	Summary of Events and Information	Remarks and references to Appendices
ARRAS	1916 7th		(continued) Sent to Noyelle Vion re models. At Mondieu an general inspection of manure dumps etc. At Ligneureuil with ADMS ascertained that Liverpool Virus rat poison contained organisms close resembling para typhoid — its use is therefore dangerous. Section making washing baths from petrol cans cut in half & reinforced with wooden battens round top rim. L/C McCoy evacuated to CCS (evacuated to Base 10.6.16). Note: Sanitation of VANQUETIN. Up to date amongst other work, over 700 loads of manure has been removed from farm yards. Between 50 + 60 barns have been cleared out & disinfected — 40 loads of rubbish removed + burnt. Ground round huts has been levelled & sown with oats, to prevent accumulation of stagnant water.	
	8th		At Hautville re barrack fatigues + construction of incinerators. At Noyelle-Vion re detailing a NCO for Sanitary work in Aveswes-le-Comte. At Ligneureuil. A.D.30 Mobile Lab. re tests on liverpool Virus — organisms found by sugar reactions to be closely allied to B.Typhosus.	
	9th		Col. Kirk to Aveswes-le-Comte. La Bareville — Saw Town Major with reference to Faeces Destructor etc. Inspected transport lines with AMQMG at Madlus, following complaints from 10th DLI.	Ela

WAR DIARY or INTELLIGENCE SUMMARY

Army Form C. 2118.

Place	Date	Hour	Summary of Events and Information	Remarks and references to Appendices
WARLUS.	1916 9th (continued) 10th	(continued)	R.A.M.C. (continued) To Hauteville saw Town Major with reference to Sanitary fatigues. To Blangermelin to inspect Baths. with it to possibility of fixing up vapour baths - found that O.C. 2nd Fd. Amb. had already got out a scheme on instructions from D.M.S. To Mazielle View re sanitary models. Called at 44th Fd. Amb. new camp at Liencourt — on to Etrée-Wamin to see new combined incinerator latrine made by 4th London Howitzer Bde. To Hauteville to lecture at Divl. Schools. To Town Major, Hauteville with reference to claim from Simencourt in connection with faeces cart. Consultation with Capt. Thompson with reference to disinfecting clothing etc of contacts of C.S.M. case at Dainville.	
	11th		Visit of Lieut Fulledam re wells - list of good wells in each village to be sent to Army Hd.Qrs. for future guidance.	
	12th		To Hauteville — saw O.C. Sirk re new incinerator. To Royal Flying Corps beyond Avesnes re construction of latrines. Sent to Mazielle View re models.	
	13th		Pte. ALLWRIGHT, No 2208, awarded 21 days Fd. Punishment. No.1, for disobedience + insolence to a N.C.O.	

Army Form C. 2118.

WAR DIARY
or
INTELLIGENCE SUMMARY
(Erase heading not required).

Instructions regarding War Diaries and Intelligence Summaries are contained in F. S. Regs., Part II. and the Staff Manual respectively. Title Pages will be prepared in manuscript.

Place	Date 1916	Hour	Summary of Events and Information	Remarks and references to Appendices
WARLUS	May (cont.) 14th	(cont.)	To Brinville saw Captain Thompson with reference to collection of infected clothing. Inspected sanitation of village in company with the medical officer.	
	15th		At Warlus on general inspection. To Hauteville for consultation with Town Mayor. To Royal Flying Corps, Avesnes-le-Comte with reference to Sharples trough.	
	16th		To Noyelle Vion re morteles. To Magnicourt. To lecture re gring.	
	17th		Visited Arras & Roville with A.D.M.S. & D.A.D.M.S. with reference to supply of coal.	
	18th		To 37th C.C.S. and Avesnes-le-Comte with A.D.M.S. & D.A.D.M.S. Inspected Bernaville. Visited Lignereuil with A.D.M.S. and D.D.M.S. with reference to material sewage scheme installation at Lignereuil.	
	19th		Inspection of trenches of R. Section with A.D.M.S.	
	20th		To Brinville & Sugar Refinery for A.D.M.S. To Hauteville & 42nd Field Ambulance	
	21st		Wrote up notes for lecture on Hygiene. To Liencourt to 4th West Ambulance inspection sanitation. Sent to Noyelle le Vion re morteles. To Brinville Schools, Hauteville	

BSD - B. M851.22/41. 12/15. 5000.

WAR DIARY
INTELLIGENCE SUMMARY

Army Form C. 2118.

Place	Date	Hour	Summary of Events and Information	Remarks and references to Appendices
WARLUS	1916 May (cont) 22		To Corps H.Q for D.D.M.S. Conference. Gave lecture on Hygiene & Sanitation at Divisional Schools.	
	23		Sgt HEATHER sent home on leave. Smoke helmet Inspection. To Hauteville re Faeces Incinerator. Inspection with S.M.O.	
	24		To Hauteville re Latrines. Sent lorry to draw empty petrol tins from Avesnes to be used. To R.E. Park, Simencourt re material for Faeces Incinerator. Sent lorry to Simencourt Station & R.E. Park. Parade of Section & fatigue men at which was read warning as to green envelopes and correspondence in France.	
	25		Wrote up notes. Saw A.A & Q.M.G re erection of tanks in trying for water supply in trenches. Visited Wanquetin re open air Swimming Bath & well for supply of Swimming Bath.	
	26		To Corps H.Q. to meet Sanitary Officer 3rd Army, with Corps D.A.D.M.S. & Sanitary Officer, 55th Division. Discussed methods of supplying clean underclothing to troops, and dealing with lice. To R.E. Park, Simencourt, re met of material for Hauteville Faeces Incinerator. Pte KEITH to Hauteville for truck on incinerator. C in C and Surgeon General visited Divisional H.Q.	

Army Form C. 2118.

WAR DIARY
or
INTELLIGENCE SUMMARY
(Erase heading not required).

Place	Date 1916	Hour	Summary of Events and Information	Remarks and references to Appendices
WARLUS	May 27th	(cont)	To Wanquetin re Baths, Horse-troughs etc. Reported on condition of horse troughs to A.D.M.S. R.E. to be requested to lay standings & arrange for drainage. Wrote up notes on Baths, Laundry, Disinfector etc. for Sanitary Officer, 3rd Army. Lorry collected linen from R.E. Park, Bernville. PTE ALLWRIGHT. F. 2208 evacuated to 37th C.C.S.	
	28th		To Wanquetin & Hauteville with A.D.M.S. & D.A.D.M.S.	
	29th		To Wanquetin re manure dump made by R.G.A. in wrong place. Saw Town Mayor with reference thereto.	
	30th		To Bernville, Wanquetin, Hauteville with A.D.M.S. & D.D.M.S. for inspection of Sanitation, Baths, Divisional Schools etc. PTE. DYER on leave. Inspected sanitation of works & wrote up notes. Visited Hauteville to inspect dumps & grease incinerator in course of erection. L/CPL HOLLIS to Arcuex - le Conte to learn district.	
	31st		To Bernville re Water supply and drainage of Mond at H.A. H.Q Qrs. To Liencourt, Lignereuil, & Arcuex - le Conte with A.D.M.S. CPL. KIRK from Arcuex - le Conte to act in Orderly Room. Lorry to R.E. Park for Ypres incinerator doors.	

E. Moseley R.E. Capt.

No. 25 San. Sect.

June 1916

COMMITTEE FOR THE
MEDICAL HISTORY OF THE WAR
5 AUG. 1916
Date

25 Sanitary Section
June 1916

Army Form C. 2118.

WAR DIARY
or
INTELLIGENCE SUMMARY
(Erase heading not required).

Instructions regarding War Diaries and Intelligence Summaries are contained in F.S. Regs., Part II, and the Staff Manual respectively. Title Pages will be prepared in manuscript.

Vol. 14

Place	Date	Hour	Summary of Events and Information	Remarks and references to Appendices
AVESNES	June 1		OC rode to AVESNES and inspected arrival of XIV Division Supply Column with G.M.O. and arranged for adjoining also Visited Corps Hd qrs & map of Corps Front. Also inspected 12th Squadron R.F.C. Camp at rear of DATES. Workshops & rode night. Corpl Kirk took charge nearly Rooms LPK FRANCIS detached to DAINVILLE.	
	2		OC inspected Trenches in Right sector of 42nd Bde Front with ADMS/XIV DIV also visited BERNEVILLE & WANQUETIN	
	3		OC inspected Left Sector, 42nd Bde Front Line Trenches occupied by KSLI with ADMS. Also visited HAUTEVILLE. Inspector brings the	
	4		OC visited DAINVILLE on inspection - sent Cpl for Refs, fees at Girls School - Lorry conveyed part from 42nd FA BARISE at HQ - PICKETT returned from HAUTEVILLE to Highsafe conducting movements line	
	5		OC relieved in sanitation at Divl School HAUTEVILLE lorry drew stores from RE Park at night. The CLEAR lead to OO pre & Church ingle Latrines	
	6		OC inspected sanitation at BERNEVILLE. Went to Corps Hdqtrs to discuss with Corps Engineer Backteriological treatment proposed for Infectious diseases Hospital LIGNEREUIL. Corpl KIRK N° 23/ promoted acting Sergeant without extra pay. Lcpl HOLLIS promoted Corpl and in charge of the CLEAR detailed for work orderly Room	
	7		OC inspected Sanitation DAINVILLE. Also went to visit School re cream of Tarts for Chlorination of drinking water. Lorry to DAINVILLE Station & RE Park	

WAR DIARY
or
INTELLIGENCE SUMMARY

(Erase heading not required).

Army Form C. 2118.

Instructions regarding War Diaries and Intelligence Summaries are contained in F. S. Regs., Part II. and the Staff Manual respectively. Title Pages will be prepared in manuscript.

Place	Date	Hour	Summary of Events and Information	Remarks and references to Appendices
Warlus	June 8th		O.C. made inspection of Warlus – Oswaega for H.d.Qs. bivouacs to dig pits and to work on removal of mud from road sides to Arras, inspected dump by incinerator site. Rode to Saurville for lunch. O.C. to Avesnes to draw more hay section — inspected sanitation of Sauquetin.	
do	9th		O.C. paid section and inspected sewage helmets — O.C. visited Berneville hay dress stores from Sauville and delivered contents.	
do	10th		O.C. visited Arras and Berneville with D.N.S. Avesnes General Office sale — Sauquetin–Pommerville —	
do	11th			
do	12th		manure dumps with Aced – Rode to R.E. Park, Station with material — Lequt. Heatol returned from leave.	
do	13th		O.C. Greaves to Hippars road and had paint for his Subalt.	
do	14th		to Sauquetin to collect site for Roofall disinfector – to Berneville to see S.O. Henry O'Billay to arrange dates for inspection of his units.	
do	15th		Sanitary Inspection of Berneville. To Wanquetin re site for faeces Destructor – requested T.M. to make an agreement with the Mayor owner for use of the land for the purpose.	

BSD-B. M351.22/41. 12/15. 5000.

WAR DIARY
or
INTELLIGENCE SUMMARY

Place	Date	Hour	Summary of Events and Information	Remarks and references to Appendices
WARLUS	June 1916 15. (continued)		To Divl. Schools, Hauteville — arranged with Capt. Benskin, R.E. to erect a model trench latrine on the modified French system with a view to its adoption in the front line.	
	16.		Inspection of Heavy Artillery in Dainville with Med. Officer. To Wanquetin + Hauteville.	
	17.		Inspected Sanitation of Hauteville — Lorry to R.E Park, Wanquetin, Arras, Dainville	
	18.		Sanitary inspection of Dainville. To O.C. R.E. Park with reference to latrine seats. Obtained prisoners for work on roads in Warlus.	
	19.		Lectured at Divl. Schools Hauteville. Writing up notes.	
	20.		Sanitary inspection of proposed trench latrine. Lorry to Avesnes-le-Comte for inspection of 5th Division. Sanitary inspection of Berneville. Consultation with Sanitary Officer.	
	21.		Officer to D.R.S. (Officers) Marin — sick. Lorry to Ligny-St-Flochel.	
	22.		Lorry to Dainville to draw stores.	
	23.		Lorry to Tincques.	
	24.		Lorry to Arras + Dainville	
	25.		Lorry to Hauteville + Wanquetin	
	26.		Officer returned from D.R.S. (Marin) — engaged on office work.	

Army Form C. 2118.

WAR DIARY
or
INTELLIGENCE SUMMARY
(Erase heading not required).

Place	Date	Hour	Summary of Events and Information	Remarks and references to Appendices
WARLUS	1916 June 27.		Inspected area in Arras taken over from 5th Division. & Hauteville to collect models. Inspected manure dumps at Wanquetin Hauteville. Dispatched St.Sergt. FULLER to 2nd. Bde. in Arras to inspect billets in Ronville. & report as to the number of fatigue required for cleaning same. & Hauteville with A.D.M.S. to inspect suggested sit of proof latrine for the trenches which has been fitted to the experimental trenches at the Schools. To St.Pol with A.D.M.S. Inspected dump Farces Incinerator at Hauteville - also manure dumps at Wanquetin Hauteville. Sent St. Sergt. Fuller to Ronville to continue his report. Lorry to Tinques.	
	28.		to Arras, Interviewed Staff Captain, 2nd Bde, with reference to cleaning cellars in Ronville. Undertook to superintend the work of the Bde. will supply the fatigue to Auesies-le-Combe & to field Cashier to M.Cor & H.Qrs. re models to Fd.Ad. Amb at Herbareq with A.D.M.S. to Linwort M.Corp HdQrs. & Avernes-le-Combe. Paid Men.	
	29.			
	30.		Acting Corp Filkins to be Acting Sergt. - Pte Eyre to be (acting) LeCorp - both promotions without extra pay.	

Murphy[?]
Capt
O/C 25[?] San Coy

15th Division

25th Sanitary Section

July 1916

COMMITTEE FOR THE
MEDICAL HISTORY OF THE WAR
Date . 5 - SEP. 1915

Army Form C. 2118.

WAR DIARY
or
INTELLIGENCE SUMMARY
(Erase heading not required).

25 Sanitary See fully vol 5

Place	Date 1916	Hour	Summary of Events and Information	Remarks and references to Appendices
WARLUS.	July 1st		BERNEVILLE evacuated. Handed over to 5th Division. S.Sergt FULLER, Corp HOLLIS, L/Cpl MARSHALL, H.J. & Pte ROGERS returned to HQrs.	MARSHALL H.J
	July 2nd		Lorry to WANQUETIN, DAINVILLE, ARRAS with stores. Inspected sanitation of 26 Mobile Vet. Section. To ARRAS re wells at ARRAS sanitation at collecting post - corner of Rue Douan. - to Candle Factory with AA QMG re complaint as to insanitary sanitation - found these had been remedied by the 6th DCLI now in occupation. Inspected latrines at Batt. HQrs. in 'SEPTEMBER' trench. Despatched S.Sergt FULLER, Corp HOLLIS, L/cpl MARSHALL H.J & Pte ROGERS + Fatigue to take over sanitary charge of DUISANS from 5th Division. Wrote up lecture Notes.	
	July 3rd		To DUISANS - settled with Town Major for horses roads for sanitary work in Village. Lectured at Divl. Schools, HAUTEVILLE. Lorry to Aveshes for inspection. Arranged for 1 NCO & 4 Men extra to report for sanitary work in DAINVILLE making BOR's in all.	
	July 4th		To R.E. Park re Stores. Inspected sanitation of Dainville. Lorry to DAINVILLE.	
	July 5th		To BERNEVILLE & MONTENESCOURT with DA.Q.M.G in search of latrine buckets left by 5th Division. Sent Horsfall destructor from WARLUS to DUISANS.	

WAR DIARY / INTELLIGENCE SUMMARY

Army Form C. 2118.

Place	Date	Hour	Summary of Events and Information	Remarks and references to Appendices
WARLUS (continued)	July 6.		To DUISANS - inspected sanitation of Battalion camp & Balloon Section etc. To ARRAS with A.D.M.S. Lorry to DAINVILLE to draw stores.	
	July 7.		Plan of Flyproof latrine for H. trenches to A.D.M.S. Inspection of suggested Flyproof latrine for front line trenches - suggested had plans - quantities prepared for proposed vapour Baths at WARLUS. for battery for R.E's to work to. Attended lecture by D.A.D.M.S. at Wanquetin. Capt. SMITH 2/17 promoted to Acting Corp with out extra pay. Lorry to DUISANS with stores.	
	July 8.		To AGNEZ with D.A.Q.M.G. to inspect dumb dumb left by 5th Division. Visited DUISANS with A.D.M.S. Held Smoke Helmet Parade.	
	July 9.		Lorry to HAUTEVILLE, WANQUETIN & DAINVILLE with stores. Represented sanitary condition of BERNEVILLE to A.A.Q.M.G. rA.D.M.S. Decided that, although mainly occupied by V Div. troops that sanitation was to be looked after by XIV Div. Rode to HAUTEVILLE to see Town Major with reference to faeces Cart for use in BERNEVILLE. Sent to AVESNES & NOYELLE-VION. Visited LATTRE ST. QUENTIN - inspected 47½ Bde RFA Wagon lines.	
	July 10.		to IGNEREUIL with A.D.M.S. re Horse manure etc. On to FREVENT to Advanced Depôt. Medical stores. To AGNEZ & VI Corps HQrs with A.D.M.S.	

Army Form C. 2118.

WAR DIARY
or
INTELLIGENCE SUMMARY
(Erase heading not required).

Instructions regarding War Diaries and Intelligence Summaries are contained in F. S. Regs., Part II. and the Staff Manual respectively. Title Pages will be prepared in manuscript.

Place	Date	Hour	Summary of Events and Information	Remarks and references to Appendices
WARLUS	July 11th		To BERNEVILLE - arranged with G.M.O. + Town Major as to fatigues from 5th Div. billeted in Village. Saw A.D.M.S. with reference to sanitation of the villages + supply of fatigues from the several Divisions in occupation. Capt. HOLLIS to BERNEVILLE to work under G.M.O. To AVESNES + VI Corps HdQrs with A.D.M.S. Lorry to DAINVILLE to collect stores.	
	July 12th		To NOYELLE-VION re withdrawal of Sergt. KIRK from AVESNES to work elsewhere. The Section is now supervising Sanitation in Arras + 10 villages + have supplied Sergts. to VI Corps HdQrs + AVESNES for the same purpose. To Sugar Factory, LOUEZ, with A.D.M.S. re complaint of insanitary condition. To DUISANS to inspect sanitation. Sanitary Inspectors of WARLUS with A.D.M.S + Town Major.	
	July 14th		To ARRAS inspecting Sanitation of Gun Positions of 46th Bde R.F.A. To 43rd F.A. A.B. HABARCQ with A.D.M.S. To LOUEZ + AGNEZ with A.D.M.S. Sent to Noyelle-Vion re models. Lorry to DAINVILLE, WANQUETIN, BEAUDICOURT + CANDAS etc.	
	July 15th		Inspected Right Sector, front line, with A.D.M.S.	
	July 16th		Inspected Sanitation of 47th Bde R.F.A. at LATTRE - ST - QUENTIN.	

WAR DIARY or INTELLIGENCE SUMMARY

Army Form C. 2118.

(Erase heading not required.)

Place	Date 1916	Hour	Summary of Events and Information	Remarks and references to Appendices
MARLUS.	July 16.		To ST NICOLAS to sample well in village (Result: 15 grs B/Powder per bucketful) + inspected trenches at ROCLINCOURT with DADMS. To AGNEZ + DUISANS.	
	July 17.		Lorry to WANQUETIN + DAINVILLE. To M Cobb HQrs to arrange with engineer for a supply of cement from 11 Cops Pk. Lectured at Divl Schools, HAUTEVILLE. Lorry to Wagnes to Coute for inspection.	
	July 18.		To AGNEZ - made inspection of village with Town Major. Made sanitary inspection of MARLUS. Lorry to DAINVILLE for stores.	
	July 19.		To AGNEZ + DUISANS. To AGNEZ + DUISANS, WANQUETIN, BERNEVILLE in afternoon. Lorry to HAUTEVILLE.	
	July 20.		Inspected sanitation of gun positions + O.P. of 47 Bde. R.F.A. with A.D.M.S. Lorry to DAINVILLE, BERNEVILLE, AGNEZ. Inspected sanitation of ARRAS with Col. BEVERIDGE, Sanitary Adviser to G.H.Q., followed by inspection of 43rd Fd. Ambulance at HABARCQ.	
	July 21.		Inspected sanitation of billets + sanitation of DUISANS. Saw DDMS with reference to Sgt. KIRK detained by 11 Corps. To Field Cashier at AVESNES to draw pay for Section.	
	July 22.		To AGNEZ re repairs to model.	
	July 23.		To AGNEZ re fatigues etc. Engaged in office on report to Col. BEVERIDGE.	

WAR DIARY or INTELLIGENCE SUMMARY

Army Form C. 2118.

Place	Date 1916	Hour	Summary of Events and Information	Remarks and references to Appendices
WARLUS	23 (continued)		Sgt. KIRK returned to Hd Qrs from AVESNES. Sent drawings & report to Col. BEVERIDGE.	
	W/24		Had marrows transplanted from HAUTEVILLE to WANQUETIN DUMP (manure). Engaged in afternoon with O.C. 11th Divl Sanitary Section — handed over maps (sanitation + water) of	
	Th/25		MOSELLY, BERNEVILLE, SIMENCOURT + WANQUETIN to him. To VI Corps. Hd Qrs with O.C. 11th Divl Sanitary Section — also to VI Corps Hd Qrs. Sent maps (sanitation + water) of WARLUS, DAINVILLE, HAUTEVILLE, + DUISANS, to D.D.M.S. VI Corps.	
	F/26		To DOULLENS with D.A.D.O.S. to buy stoves, etc. To AGNEZ + HAUTEVILLE with A.D.M.S.	
	S/27		Consultation with Sanitary Officer 21 Division, A.D's M.S. 21 + 11 Divisions. To DUISANS + AGNY with instructions for Sub-Sections. Wired instructions with various Sub-Sections to join up with Brigades — arranged with O.C. Trains, Staff Major R.E., for Sanitary Sub-Sections to supervise sanitation of safe walks. Sent lorry with gear for Baths to Sub. St. LEGER. Sr. Sergt. FULLER, L/c MARSHALL A.L, Pte ROGERS from DUISANS reported to 42nd Bde for duty. (Corps. Smith from HAUTEVILLE dtto) Pte. PATTON from HAUTEVILLE returned to Hd Qrs.	
	Tu/28		Sergt. AXWELL L/c CLARK MARSHALL from ARRAS reported to 42nd Bde for duty — (Pte. HATTON dtto.) 71 IN + AGNEZ.	

WAR DIARY
or
INTELLIGENCE SUMMARY

Army Form C. 2118.

(Erase heading not required.)

Place	Date 1916	Hour	Summary of Events and Information	Remarks and references to Appendices
WARLUS.	July 29.		To AGNEZ re movement of Fd. Bde. To DUISANS with ADMS to interview ADMS 11th Division. Wired OC 11th Div. Sanitary Section that Stores awaited him at WARLUS, & requesting him to take over.	
SUS ST. LEGER.	July 30.		Evacuated WARLUS. Pack Section Lorry to SUS ST. LEGER. Lorry to WANQUETIN, AGNEZ, Grand RULLECOURT, SUS ST. LEGER to take down mobile Lorry to LOUEZ. Removed Bath apparatus from SUS ST. LEGER & taken to LOUEZ. Lorry to collect Bath apparatus (Dumbed at SUS ST. LEGER). Made enquiries with A.D.M.S as to collection sterilization of water in SUS ST. LEGER	
FROHEN-le-Grand. (Somme-Pas-de-)	July 31.		Pack Section Lorry from SUS ST. LEGER to FROHEN-le-PETIT.	

EMurihi Rlu
Cap/
1/8/16 OC 2/5 Sanitary Section
11th Division

14th Dns

No. 25. Sanitary Section

August, 1916

COMMITTEE FOR THE
MEDICAL HISTORY OF THE WAR
Date -5 OCT. 1916

Army Form C. 2118.

WAR DIARY
or
INTELLIGENCE SUMMARY

(Erase heading not required).

2nd San Sec
Vol 16

Place	Date	Hour	Summary of Events and Information	Remarks and references to Appendices
BERNAVILLE (SOMME)	August 1916 1.		Pvt Seehow lorry to BERNAVILLE. Latrines erected at Batts. two water reconnaissance made of village.	
	2.		Sanitarian repaired latrines erected at Noo Ness. Interviewed Mayor with reference to general sanitation of village — borrowed map of village — ¹⁰/⁵⁰⁰⁰⁰ used after tracing. Saw Authorities with reference to hire of water cart — to DOULLENS on same errand — (BERNAVILLE water cart requisitioned by Military Authorities for DOULLENS). Water map prepared of BERNAVILLE village. Smoke helmet inspection. General supervision of sanitation in village. Arranged for fatigues for road sweeping, watering. General supervision of sanitation in village.	
	3. 4. 5. 6.		(to DOULLENS to purchase stores (to DOULLENS to buy measures for chlorinating (to No 3 C.C.S. for A.D.M.S. small quantities of water.	
Now BUIRE-sur-l'Ancre.	7.		Lorry took Section to camp between RIBEMONT-sur-l'ANCRE + BUIRE-sur-l'Ancre. Position D⁹⁺⁹ & 4.c. (Sheet Albert) (to IV Army Park to enquire re material. (, BUIRE, DERNANCOURT, VIVIERS Mill re. bivouac boots. (3. last named place with A.D.M.S.). Took Sergt. HAXELL to VIVIERS Mill wt. a view to his taking charge of the Batts. Bivouacs were erected.	
	8.		Section employed on improvements to Sanitary arrangements of HdQrs. camp. Erected Aldik⁸ Beach Pump, improved 3 latrines, made 2 new latrines.	

WAR DIARY or INTELLIGENCE SUMMARY

Army Form C. 2118.

Place	Date August	Hour	Summary of Events and Information	Remarks and references to Appendices
BUIRE-sur-l'Ancre	8 (contd.)		Arranged with OC. 17 Div. Salvage Coy. for fatigues to DERNANCOURT. (for Brigade) Sent for materials to No.6 R.E. Park. — Timber obtained from Corps Park (Dump)	
	9.		Erected drinking water pump in HQrs camp. To HQrs 17 Division to see OC. San. Sec. previous to taking over. Went to Baths at VIVIERS MILL — no apparatus had arrived.	
	10.		To HEILLY wt DADMS. To VIVIERS MILL re Baths. to 1 Bde HQrs. re sanitation of DERNANCOURT. Section making 500 crosses for Div. Chaplain. Div. Sanitary Column undertook to make at 63 Coy. measures for chlorination of water for trenches	
	11.		Rn. DAWSON. No 9289 made Act. L. Cpl. Male employed with 25 Sanitary Section. Sergt. KIRK No 937 to xv Corps. Res. Station. The crosses completed. New N.C.Os latrine fitted up. to VIVIER's MILL re Baths General inspection of sanitation of BUIRE + DERNANCOURT.	
	12.		Sent Pte. CLEAL to new HQrs S.E. of ALBERT to take over Stores from 17 Div. San. Sec. to BELLE VUE FARM. to see O.C. 17 Div. San. Sec. at Section moved to BELLE VUE FARM. (S.E. of ALBERT.)	
BELLE VUE FARM (S.E. of ALBERT)	13.		Sprayed tents, dug-outs + Mo. Mess. Inspected Carsof 3rd Div. Train. to FRICOURT re water + HAMET to Adv. Dressing Stn. with ADMS	

Army Form C. 2118.

WAR DIARY
or
INTELLIGENCE SUMMARY
(Erase heading not required.)

Place	Date	Hour	Summary of Events and Information	Remarks and references to Appendices
BELLE VUE FARM. (Sd. ALBERT).	August 14.		To Aid Post re Chartres Wd. ADMS re 4th Fd. Ambulance — arranged to send 10 Formalin to office and for dangerous water. (to ADQRs. 33rd Divl. Sanitary Section re boundaries to Sanitary area etc. Sent Cpl. HOLLIS to instruct men as to treatment of manure.	
	15.		To BÉCORDEL - BÉCOURT re sanitation round watering point wtg/ing of sub-section of 43 Brigade. To 4th Fd. Amb. 4th Bridgade Hd Qrs wt ADMS. To No 3 CCS re Sayers stoves. Reorganised work of sections in accordance wt. N Army instructions as to Sanitary areas. Withdrew sub-sections from 4/1 Brigades related 1/3 4 Divl. Area to each sub-section. Lorry to Divl. Dump at RICOURT for stores. Reinforcements arrived (Pte. HIGGINS No. 3132, Pte. CROPPER No. 3242)	
	16.		Lorry to Divl. Dump at RICOURT. Wt RE RK RIBEMONT, for stores. Cpl. SMITH to Sgt. BAILEY'S sub-section to replace Cpl. HOLLIS — the latter to join Sgt. FULLER'S sub-section. Inspected camps at W. end of new sanitary area wt. ADMS. Wrote sanitary circular for issue to Divl. Units. Visited BÉCORDEL-BÉCOURT — arranged for chlorination of all water issued to watercarts + gadilings from water point. Inspected dry bed of stream between BÉCORDEL-BÉCOURT + MÉAULTE. Found sanitary very bad — refuse tins, tyler rubbish, littering bottom of stream + latrines belonging to	

WAR DIARY or INTELLIGENCE SUMMARY

Army Form C. 2118.

Place	Date	Hour	Summary of Events and Information	Remarks and references to Appendices
BELLE-VUE FARM. (S.E. of ALBERT)	August 1916 16		(continued) units actually dug in to stream bed. — instructed Sgt-Major J D/9 Bde RFA to clean out bed of stream at back of his horse lines. Air fix native boards to prohibit washing in the stagnant pools. Made a further 200 crosses for DAQMG. 20 Div.	
	17.		Prepared 3 maps of Dvl. Sanitary areas made 12 direction boards for aid posts in trenches for ADMS. Pte. CROPPER N:3242 t. water bowl at BÉCORDEL. Rode round Sanitary areas with NO. y e Sub-Areas. 1. No 3 CCS for covers. Gave for use of 49 Fld. Amb. Arranged for 2 men from 49th Fld. Amb to take charge of water chlorination at FRICOURT.	
	18.		To No 6 RE Park to arrange for supply of materials. 1. Adv Dressing Stn inf ADMS. with DADMS re Baths at VINER'S Mill. 1. Adv. Dressing Stn inf ADMS. Sent a fly proof latrines to No 8 MAC. Section 1. to Sgt. FULLER 91 Public latrines in MAMETZ. Made 13 fly proof latrine' seats for MAMETZ. To FRICOURT re public latrines "MAMETZ.	
	19.		To baths at VINER'S Mill — to 11th Kings Liverpool Reg. re. chlorination of water at water point. Lorry to FRICOURT - BÉCORDEL with stores Re. case of bacillary diarrhoea. Arrangements made for Sgt. HAXELLE Sub. Section 1. to M/Car Dvl. Train. Pte. HUGGINS N⁰ 3152 t. water point at BÉCORDEL to join Pte. CROPPER N⁰ 3242.	

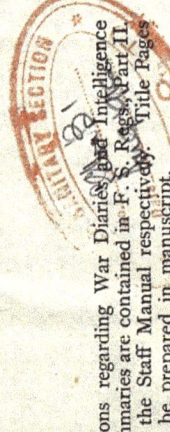

WAR DIARY
or
INTELLIGENCE SUMMARY

(Erase heading not required.)

Army Form C. 2118.

Place	Date	Hour	Summary of Events and Information	Remarks and references to Appendices
BELLE-VUE FARM. (S.E. of ALBERT).	August 1916. 20.		Inspected No.1 Area. Instructed Pte. CROPPER i/c water point at BECORDEL in duties in connection with watercarts. Sent 4 pikable incinerators to Sgt. BAILEY for use in Back Area — also 5 to Sgt. HAXELL for use in Middle Area.	
	21.		Visited S/Sgt. FULLER i/c No.3 Area. To water point at FRICOURT with reference to small tanks for filling 2gall petrol cans. To Adv. Dressing Stn. Inspected Camps in middle back area. To AMIENS to purchase stores. Lorry to MAMETZ & FRICOURT with stores.	
	22.		To MAMETZ to inspect progress of latrines etc. (4 for Forward Area). Inspected camp of 26 Mobile Vet. Section at RIBEMONT. To Adv. Dressing Stn. Made 3 more incinerators for middle area.	
	23.		Inspected MAMETZ. Thicks in middle area — returned Soyers stove borrowed from C.C.S. Lorry to FRICOURT for stores. Erected Public Urinal outside Canteen of 8th M.M.G Section — erected 2 incinerators at Ad.Qrs. Smoke helmet Parade.	
	24.		General inspection of camps around H.Qrs. Lorry to FRICOURT for stores. Erected ablution bench & shed for Ad.Qrs. Sent Sgt. BAILEY & extra incinerators for use in back area. Detailed 6 men to Baths at MIER'S Mill on instructions from A.D.M.S.	

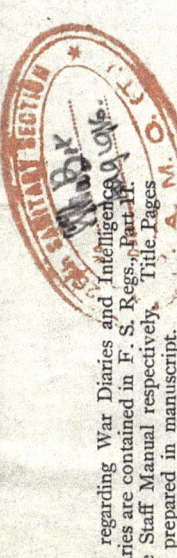

Army Form C. 2118.

WAR DIARY
or
INTELLIGENCE SUMMARY
(Erase heading not required.)

Place	Date	Hour	Summary of Events and Information	Remarks and references to Appendices
BELLE VUE FARM (S.E. P. ALBERT)	Aug 1916 25.		4 RIBEMONT to 26 Mobile Vet. Section. To Baths at VIVIERS MILL. During afternoon was informed that a reinforcement camp was to be pitched near Hd Qrs & asked to lay it out. Obtained a fatigue party & set all available Section men to work. By dark 1 Officers latrine (2 seater), 1 Mens latrine (10 seater), Ablution Bench & Shed, Urine Trough, & grease trap were ready. Sent to FRICOURT for materials. Withdrew Pte. CLEAL from Baths seek Pte. ROGERS to replace him.	
	26.		Consultation with Sanitary Officer 33rd Division on condition of quarry, chlorination of water at filling points etc., etc.. Inspection of camps in Back area. Sent to No 6 RE Park for materials.	
	27.		Office work in morning - writing up notes. In afternoon inspected camp of No 11 Wks Balloon Section reported to ADMS. Lorry to FRICOURT for materials.	
	28.		Sent to No 6 RE Park for stoves. Had a survey made of condition & equipment of all watercarts filling at BECORDEL forks. Inspected Hd Qrs camp 25 Division who which it was said had to use Dw. water points at FRICOURT & BECORDEL.	
	29.		Visited water points at FRICOURT & BECORDEL. Pte. FRANCIS to 42 Fd. Ambulance Sick. Had a similar survey made of watercarts at FRICOURT forks as at BECORDEL. To Nr. 26 Mobile Vet. Section.	

Army Form C. 2118.

WAR DIARY
or
INTELLIGENCE SUMMARY

(Erase heading not required.)

Instructions regarding War Diaries and Intelligence Summaries are contained in F.S. Regs., Part II. and the Staff Manual respectively. Title Pages will be prepared in manuscript.

Place	Date	Hour	Summary of Events and Information	Remarks and references to Appendices
BELLE-VUE FARM (S.E. of ALBERT)	Aug 30 1916.		Reported to ADMS on surveys made at waterpoints at PRICOURT BECORDEL. Arranged for Sub-Sections to rejoin Brigades. Sgt. BAILEY, Cpl. SMITH, Pte. MACKAY + HUGGINS to 41st L.F. Bde. S.Sgt. FILLER, Cpl. HOLLIS, L/Cpl. MARSHALL A.J. + Pte. ROGERS to 42nd L.F. Bde. Sgt. MAXELL, Corps CLARK + MARSHALL C., + Pte. HATTON to 43rd L.F. Bde. Sgt. FILKINS + L/Cpl. EYRE to remain with "A" Bde. 19 Bde. RFA to supervise sanitation of RFA. Engaged all day on office work.	
BELLOY. (W. of AMIENS)	31.		Pak Section by train from ALBERT to BELLOY. — Lorry with Section gear by road.	

E. Moorlake
Capt.
O.C. 25th Sanitary Section
XIV Division.

[Stamp: 25th SANITARY SECTION, Date Aug 31/1916, R.A.M.C. (T.)]

140/134

14th (Light) Divn

No. 25 Sanitary Section

COMMITTEE FOR THE
MEDICAL HISTORY OF THE WAR
Date 26 OCT 1915

WAR DIARY
INTELLIGENCE SUMMARY

Army Form C. 2118.

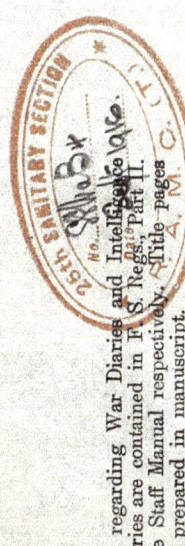

Place	Date	Hour	Summary of Events and Information	Remarks and references to Appendices
BELLOY	September 1st		Attended x Corps Conference at LONG with A.D.M.S. General inspection of village. Put section making flyproof latrine boxes. Erected permanent latrines for officers & men in Sanitary Section Camp. Made flyproof latrine box - vinned of H.Qrs. Divl. train. Tested 2 Public wells - no chloride of lime needed.	
	2nd		Pte. FRANCIS No. 1934 evacuated to C.C.S - sick. Sent 5 Flyproof latrines to H.Qrs. & 2 to Divl. Signal Coy. Erected a similar seat over latrine bucket in No. 2 Mess. Made 3 portable incinerators & erected same for use in village. Inspection of village & arranged sanitary conveniences. Sent lorry to BURE to collect bat apparatus - delivered me set to 43 Bde. H.Qrs. Visited BOISRAULT - 43rd Fd. Ambulance.	
	3rd		Visited BOISRAULT & HORNOY with A.D.M.S. re erection of Baths - sent 1 set of Baths to 42 & 43 Bde. for erection in Bde. Area. Made 2 flyproof latrines for H.Qrs. Sent stoves to Sergt. Bailey & Sergt. Havell. Lorry to Refilling Point for 50 lbs. biscuit boxes.	
	4th		General inspection of village. Go 42 Inf. Bde. H.Qrs. re erection of Baths. Made 2 latrines for Hd. Qrs.	
	5th		Conference of ADMS with Regimental M.O's - afterwards conducted them round village & showed them examples of the various sanitary appliances in use - discussed anti fly measures etc.	

Army Form C. 2118.

WAR DIARY
or
INTELLIGENCE SUMMARY
(Erase heading not required.)

Instructions regarding War Diaries and Intelligence Summaries are contained in F. S. Regs., Part VII. and the Staff Manual respectively. Title Pages will be prepared in manuscript.

Place	Date 1916	Hour	Summary of Events and Information	Remarks and references to Appendices
BELLOY.	September 5. (continued)		Reported to A.D.M.S. on advisability of setting up a workshop for construction of sanitary appliances. Officer to LE TREPORT on two days' leave. Also sealer fly proof latrine + urinal erected for D.A.D.O.S.	
	6.		2 made for Hd.Qrs. – erected a fly proof latrine + urinal for A.D.M.S. Sent escort to AMIENS to fetch Pte. KEITH 23656 from guard room - charged by A.P.M. Amiens with being drunk at 5 p.m. Sent cresol to Batts. at 43rd Bde. Hd.Qrs. Lorry to HANGAST Sta. with party. Incinerators made for 41 + 43 Bde. Hd.Qrs.	
			1 Incinerator to 6 S.L.I. – made fly proof door of gauze for No 2 Mess Kitchen. 1 Incinerator to Sgt Bailey for 41 W. Bde. Notice boards to to 3 Sub Sections. Lorry to HORNOY + ABBEVILLE.	
	8.		1 Incinerator, a 3 seater latrine + 3 Separate latrines to Sgt. Bailey. Lorry to HORNOY + ABBEVILLE with dirty linen.	
	9.		Officer returned from LE TREPORT. Sent lorry to EPAUMESNIL to 42 Bde. Batts. for clothing. Pte KEITH awarded 28 days F.P. No 2 for being drunk in AMIENS or Public Urinal in main street outside Estaminet. Made + erected a map of METIGNY showing sanitary arrangements.	
			Lorry to ABBEVILLE. Prepared a map of BELLOY.	
	10.		Sketched a similar plan of BELLOY. General inspection of village. Lorry to HORNOY + ABBEVILLE with clean dirty linen. (No 3 C.C.S.) to arrange loan of Sayers stove if needed.	
Near BUIRE-sur-l'Ancre.	11.		Lorry + Pst. Section "toured" BELLOY to camp between RIBEMONT + BUIRE.	

Army Form C. 2118.

WAR DIARY
or
INTELLIGENCE SUMMARY
(Erase heading not required.)

Instructions regarding War Diaries and Intelligence Summaries are contained in F. S. Regs., Part I. & II. and the Staff Manual respectively. Title Pages will be prepared in manuscript.

Place	Date	Hour	Summary of Events and Information	Remarks and references to Appendices
Near BUIRE-sur-l'ANCRE	Sept. 1916 11. (Cont)		Sprayed out Men Mess. General Inspection of camp. Sent report list of sanitary conveniences, permanents, semi-permanent, to DDMS & Corps & ADMS.	
	12.		General Inspection of camp. Inspected bomb sanitation of 42 Bde. in reserve camp near DERNANCOURT. Inspected camp at E.13.a (Albert Sheet 57D.SD.) just vacated by 41 Inf. Bde. Lorry to Refilling Point Supply Column for 2 gall. petrol cans for 41 Inf. Bde. Sent lorry to collect 5 tents from Heavy Artillery HdQrs for use of Divl HdQrs at FRICOURT Chateau.	
FRICOURT CHATEAU	13.		To new HdQrs at FRICOURT CHATEAU. Lorry to BUIRE + BELLE-VUE-FARM. (N. ALBERT) for HdQrs kits. By motor to A.D.S. with Serjt. Healter + Pte. Cooper (Bernafay Wood) - proceeded on foot to test wells in LONGUEVAL - meeting with heavy bombardment in DELVILLE Wood at entrance to LONGUEVAL which showed no signs of abating - postponed tests till another day. Inspected HdQrs camp at FRICOURT CHATEAU.	
	14.		Inspected sanitation at FRICOURT camp occupied by 42 Bde + details. To Adv. H.Q. 141st Fld. Ambulance at A.D.M.S. Inspected sanitation at DERNANCOURT camp occupied by 43rd Inf. Bde. Despatched Pte. HATTON Pte. HUGGINS & BECORDEL for duty at water point. Sprayed dugouts at FRICOURT Chateau.	
	15.		To MONTAUBAN with A.D.M.S. re Public Latrines etc. To Divl. Collecting Stn. - arranged for lorry	

Army Form C. 2118.

WAR DIARY
or
INTELLIGENCE SUMMARY

(Erase heading not required.)

Place	Date 1916	Hour	Summary of Events and Information	Remarks and references to Appendices
FRICOURT Chateau	September 15 (Continued)		to take timber to Fd place for erection of additional shelters & to bring back a load of light wounded with Y Corps. Dressing Stn. to LONGUEVAL to locate wells Rest water with Sergt. HEATHER Pte. CROPPER. — Found 1 well — approximately 300 ft. deep and no lifting apparatus.	
	16.		Lorry to REILLY for Stretchers to Adv. Dressing Stn. to convey light wounded to Y Corps. Dressing Stn. General inspection of camp. Reported to ADMS re wells in LONGUEVAL. To 44th Fd. Amb. & inspected FRICOURT camp — noticed dirty condition in which ground had been left by Units in 21 Division — reported same to H.Qrs. Lorry to Rd Park for stores.	
near BUIRE sur l'ANCRE	17.		Pd. Section & Lorry (3 journeys) from FRICOURT to camp between BUIRE RIBEMONT General Inspection of camp. To VIVIERS MILL to take over charge of Corps Baths. reported to A.D.M.S. number of personnel required to work the Baths. — saw Sergt. Ye Baths.	
	18.		To VIVIERS MILL to Baths. (2 Fd Ambulance to arrange for S.Sergt. FULLERS arrest + transport to Orderly Rm	
	19.		S. Sergt. FULLER brought to H.Qrs. San. Sec under arrest to answer a charge of "Conduct to the prejudice of good order & Military discipline in that he at HORNOY Somme le 19/16 by threats + abusive language induced or attempted to induce W/M 65229 Dr. RADCLIFFE R. to disobey his orders by carrying an excessive number of passengers in his motor ambulance.	

Army Form C. 2118.

WAR DIARY or INTELLIGENCE SUMMARY

(Erase heading not required.)

Place	Date 1916	Hour	Summary of Events and Information	Remarks and references to Appendices
Near Buire-sur-l'Ancre	September 19 (continued)		The accused asked for a court-martial. To UMERS MILL. General inspection of camp.	
	20.		Statement & evidence for court-martial of Sergt. FULLER taken. Forwarded to O' Office who, on consideration of evidence, recommended that he accused be discharged on the grounds of "insufficient evidence" adding that he should be warned to be more careful of his conduct in future. 5 fly-proof latrine seats + 1 incinerator sent to 49 Bde. H.Qrs. 7 proof latrine seats + 2 incinerators sent to 41 Bde. H.Qrs. General inspection, supervision of sanitary work in H.Qrs. camp. Officer confined to his bed. General supervision of sanitary work.	
	21.		Officer confined to his bed. General supervision of sanitary work. Lorry to DOULLENS (Linda) for A.D.M.S.	
La CLAIROY.	22.		Lorry (journey 3) + back section to La CLAIROY.	
	23.		Tested & labelled wells in village - Plated locations & water sources on map. Village supplied by III Corps. Officer to III Corps H.Q. to MARLUS in fruitless errands to meet C. Sanitary section to Division. Pat Section making portable incinerators. Sent H+poof Latrine seat to 49 Bde. Hd. Qrs.	

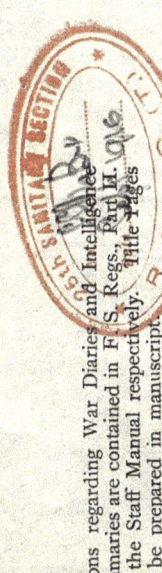

2449 Wt. W14957/M90 750,000 1/16 J.B.C. & A. Forms/C.2118/12.

WAR DIARY or INTELLIGENCE SUMMARY

Army Form C. 2118.

Place	Date	Hour	Summary of Events and Information	Remarks and references to Appendices
1st CURDY.	September 1916 24.		Erected officers latrines.	
	25.		to WARLUS to see OC Sanitary Section, 12th Division to 43 Bde. H.Q. at SUS. ST. LEGER. Lorry to Railhead for rations to Railhead for D.A.D.O.S. OC Sankay Section 12 Division to arrange handing over + detailing squads to 3 villages. Lorry to LUCHEUX, GRAND RULLECOURT, SUS. ST. LEGER to fix up Sub-Sections from to Brigades + transported.
			Sgt. MAXELL. Sgt. BAILEY. Cpl. ALLIS.
			L/Cpl. MARSHALL.C. C/S. SMITH. L/Cpl. MARSHALL H.J.
			L/Cpl. CLARK. Pte. MACKAY. Pte. ROGERS.
			Pte. HATTON. Pte. HIGGINS.
GOUY. WARLUS.	26.		Lorry to GOUY, BEAUMETZ-les-LOGES, BERNEVILLE to BEAUMETZ-les-LOGES to GOUY. BERNEVILLE taking sanitary fatigues of 1 NCO + 6 men to each Place. Pack Section + lorry to WARLUS. Officer to GOUY with D.H.Q. Officer to WARLUS to BERNEVILLE + BEAUMETZ on inspection. 1 Cpl. CHECKLEY to AVESNES-le-Comte.
	27.		General inspection of GOUY. Officer indisposed. Inspected sanitarium of WARLUS. Visit a view to taking over from 12th Division. Sgt. Maxell + L/Cpl. CLARK to ARRAS to supervise sanitation. Reinforcements arrived. Pte. SMITH. E.V 99. Pte. GORDON. I.M. 767 (arrived in GOUY 20 Sept/16).
WARLUS.	28.		Officer to WARLUS. Took village over from 12th Division.

Army Form C. 2118.

WAR DIARY
or
INTELLIGENCE SUMMARY
(Erase heading not required.)

Place	Date	Hour	Summary of Events and Information	Remarks and references to Appendices
WARLUS.	September 1916. 28 (continued)		Pte. CHEAL T.A. 9969 & Pte. CROPPER J.E. 3240 to be L/Cpls without extra pay.	
	29.		Officer on leave to England. General inspection of village. Erected new incinerator at disposal ground. S/Sgt FULLER 2119 returned from XV Corps HQrs to Goury. Made arrangements to send, on to 30th inst, the following men to :— S/Sgt FULLER to ACHICOURT to supervise sanitation of AGNY, ACHICOURT. Sgt. Bailey & Pte. Mackay to SIMENCOURT — SIMENCOURT & BEAUMETZ-les-Loges. Cpl. SMITH & Pte. HIGGINS to 4th Bde HQrs — WAILLY, RIVIERE, BRETENCOURT, GROSVILLE & FERMONT	
	30.		Paid men. General inspection of village.	

140/1811

14th Div.

Oct. 1916

25th Sanitary Section.

COMMITTEE FOR THE
MEDICAL HISTORY OF THE WAR
Date -9 DEC. 1916

Army Form C. 2118.

WAR DIARY or INTELLIGENCE SUMMARY
(Erase heading not required.)

Place	Date 1916	Hour	Summary of Events and Information	Remarks and references to Appendices
WARLUS (continued)	Oct 1.		Cleaned out water tanks at No. 9 Rue de Dainville (Well No. 19). Inspection of village with G.M.O. Sent stores to BEAUMETZ-les-Loges. Arranged site of manure dump on Manqueture Rd. Lorry to Refilling Point + LARBRET for stores.	
	2.		Well No. 19 out of repair — reported same to C.R.E.	
	3.		Erected night urinal stands outside Estaminet No. 2 Rue de Dainville. General inspection of village. Lorry to Workshops for inspection + LARBRET for stores. General sanitary inspection of village. Sprayed out 2 rooms of No. 13 Rue d'Agnes (Measles case). Erected 1 latrine + 2 public urinals. Remodelled 1 latrine. Lorry to Refilling Point.	
	4.		General sanitary inspection of village. Erected 1 public dump + remodelled 1 Public latrine. Lorry to Berneville with stores.	
	5.		General sanitary inspection of village. Remodelled 1 Public Urinal. Sent 1 load of scrap wood to SIMENCOURT. Stores to RIVIERE + BERNEVILLE. Lorry to GOUY-IZEL-le-HAMEAU. Water tanks (No. 19 well) again in order.	
	6.		General inspection of village with G.M.O. Fatigue party (6 O.R.s) reported from Town Major WARLUS.	

Army Form C. 2118.

WAR DIARY
or
INTELLIGENCE SUMMARY
(Erase heading not required.)

Place	Date October 1916	Hour	Summary of Events and Information	Remarks and references to Appendices
WARLUS (continued)	6 (cont.)		Remodelled 1 latrine.	
	7.		Lorry to GOUY - IZEL-le-HAMEAU	
	8.		General Sanitary inspection of village. Remodelled 2 latrines. General sanitary inspection of village. Erected 1 officers latrine. Sent stores to AGNY, SIMENCOURT.	
	9.		Made arrangements to place water tank platform out of bounds to unauthorized persons to prevent drinking water being drawn for ablution purposes (No9 well). Remodelled H.Q. & Qr. Mens' latrine. Lorry to AVESNES for stores.	
	10.		General inspection of village. Lorry to AVESNES (2) LARBRET Refilling Pt. Erected a cutter Refuse dump.	
	11.		No/A ERE to AVESNES to replace Pte. CHECKLEY on leave. Erected public latrine in Band Sord. - sent stores to BEAUMETZ & RIVIERE. General inspection of village. Lorry to LARBRET for stores, & to BERNEVILLE with stores.	
	12.		General inspection of village. Remodelled 2 latrines. Made good ablution bench to Band Sord. Lorry to AVESNES & LARBRET for stores for O.C. Baths. Stores to BERNEVILLE.	

Army Form C. 2118.

WAR DIARY
or
INTELLIGENCE SUMMARY
(Erase heading not required.)

Instructions regarding War Diaries and Intelligence Summaries are contained in F. S. Regs., Part II. and the Staff Manual respectively. Title Pages will be prepared in manuscript.

Place	Date October 1916	Hour	Summary of Events and Information	Remarks and references to Appendices
WARLUS (cont)	13.		General inspection of village with G.M.O. Cleaned out watertanks. Remodelled 2 latrines. Stores to ARRAS, ACHICOURT, RIVIERE, SIMENCOURT, BEAUMETZ & BERNEVILLE.	
	14.		Lorry to GOUY for coal to AVESNES for linen. General inspection of village. Remodelled 2 latrines. Sent stores to BERNEVILLE.	
	15.		General inspection of village with G.M.O. Remodelled 3 latrines. Made 1 greasetrap for No.3 Mess. Officer returned from leave.	
	16.		General inspection of WARLUS. Greasetraps dug at 89 Cy R.E. billet & C.R.A. Office work. To BEAUMETZ on sanitary inspection. Lorry to AVESNES for clean linen to BEAUMETZ RIVIERE with stores.	
	17.		General inspection of BERNEVILLE. Alterations & additions to No.2 Mess. Remodelled 1 latrine. To AVESNES for stores A.P.C. Office. Took over charge of San. Dis. Baths from Capt. Brown, R.A.M.C.	
	18.		Inspected SIMENCOURT. Received certificate from Major of WANQUETIN re. results of treatment of manure in relation to reduction of fly-pest during summer months. Lorry to AVESNES for linen & to Refilling Point. Erected latrine at C.R.A. billet.	

Army Form C. 2118.

WAR DIARY
or
INTELLIGENCE SUMMARY
(Erase heading not required.)

Place	Date	Hour	Summary of Events and Information	Remarks and references to Appendices
WARLUS (cont)	19.		Lorry to AVESNES, BERNEVILLE, RIVIERE, BEAUMETZ with stores. Also to Refilling Pt. Made grease trap at 89 Fld Co RE 2nd Cookhouse. Remodelled 1 latrine. To BEAUMETZ SIMENCOURT on inspection.	
	20.		Lorry to Avesnes Refilling Pt., to DAINVILLE for sawdust. Closed baths at Le FERMONT DAINVILLE + reduced bathing arrangements at ARRAS to 3 days per week. To BARLY to arrange for Sanitary Sgt. (A/Lgt Filkins) to supervise sanitation of FOSSEUX + BARLY under to G.M.O. To AVESNES to purchase stores for Baths.	
	21.		Lorry to Refilling Pt, GOUY, Lt. SIMENCOURT for stores. Inspection of RIVIERE Le FERMONT including Baths. Attended DDMS Conference VI Corps.	
	22.		Lorry to Avesnes Refilling Pt. Remodelled 1 latrine. General inspection of village. Baths at SIMENCOURT + BERNEVILLE closed to XIII Division from 23rd inst. now referred to XII Division without issue of clean clothing. To WAILLY inspected 11 Kings Liverpools + 41 Bde M.G.Coy — to FOSSEUX inspected D.A.C. with	

Army Form C. 2118.

WAR DIARY
or
INTELLIGENCE SUMMARY

(Erase heading not required.)

Place	Date Oct 1916	Hour	Summary of Events and Information	Remarks and references to Appendices
WARLUS	22. (continued)		ADMS. To BARLY.	
	23.		Inspected WARLUS - Interviewed Capt. Longstone, XII Divl. San. Sec. with a view to their taking over Area. Erected a new mens latrine at HQrs cookhouse.	
	24.		Inspected SIMENCOURT. Visited Baths at 4 Fd. Amb re bathing men of HQrs Train + D.A.C.	
	25.		To Laundry at AVESNES. Made arrangements for Sub Sections to join up with W. Bdes. during move. General inspection of WARLUS. Interviewed CRE. re Baths.	
			Sent Batt. personnel back to various Fld. Ambs. Sent 2 loads of Stores to GRAND RULLECOURT.	
	26.		To Laundry at AVESNES.	
			To AVESNES to arrange site for Foden lorry.	
Le CAUROY	27.		Rail Section lorry to Le CAUROY. To AVESNES to obtain Store for clean clothing.	
			To MATONG re Cartage of clothing from AMIENS.	
	28.		To AMIENS to settle Laundry A/c. Lorry drew 2000 shirts from AMIENS Laundry.	
			Sent stores to 41 Bde. (Sgt. Bailey)	
	29.		To Laundry AVESNES re Stock of clothing. — To Town Major re clothing stores.	
			Lorry to LARBRET Refilling Pt. for stores. Erected 1 Officers latrine & Urinal at No.1 Mess.	
	30.		Inspected 43 Bde. HQrs. + 10 D.L.I. at AMBRIN. + 42 Bde HQrs + M.G.Coy at LIENCOURT. Lorry to LARBRET for stores for 13 Fld. Amb. at GIVENCHY-le-Noble.	
			Sent stores to 4 Bde HQrs. Erected 1 mens latrine behind No.2 Mess.	

Army Form C. 2118.

WAR DIARY
or
INTELLIGENCE SUMMARY

(Erase heading not required.)

Instructions regarding War Diaries and Intelligence Summaries are contained in F. S. Regs., Part II. and the Staff Manual respectively. Title Pages will be prepared in manuscript.

Place	Date	Hour	Summary of Events and Information	Remarks and references to Appendices
Le CAUROY	October 1916 31.		Inspected Hd Qrs - 'C' Coy D.C.L.I. To PREVENT re site of Foden Lorry etc. To Laundry at AVESNES. Sent stores to 43 Bde. Hd Qrs.	

Shoppi Ril
Capt.
OC 25 Sanitary Section
XII Division

Noser 916.

Confidential

War Diary

of

25th Sanitary Section

for

month of

November 1916

WAR DIARY or INTELLIGENCE SUMMARY

Army Form C. 2118.

Place	Date November 1916	Hour	Summary of Events and Information	Remarks and references to Appendices
Le Cauroy	1st		To AVESNES to Foden lorry & Laundry. Office work.	
	2nd		To IZEL-e-HAMEAU. Inspected 2 Coys 6 DCLI. To LIENCOURT in search of clean clothing store. To LIGNEREUIL to Corps Med Schools re lectures. Lorry to LARBRET + Refilling Point.	Lect over BERLENCOURT Baths Nov 7/1916
	3rd		To AVESNES to Laundry + to LIENCOURT re clothes store. Office work. Lorry to LARBRET Refilling Point.	
	4th		To AVESNES to Laundry. To LIENCOURT re clothes store - saw Town Major. Working up lecture notes. Lectured at Corps Med Schools LIGNEREUIL. To FREVENT re site of Foden lorry at Chateau, in view of removal of the laundry to that place.	
	5th		Lectured at Corps Med Schools. To Laundry at AVESNES. To SUS-ST-LEGER to find clothes store. Inspected sanitation of Le Cauroy. Office work.	
	6th		Lectured at Corps Med Schools. To BEAUFORT to see OC Devons re clothing at BERLENCOURT Baths. OC absent. To SUS-ST-LEGER to measure up barn for clothing store.	
	7th		To GRAND RULLECOURT - inspected sanitation of Divl Schools. Lectured at Corps Med Schools. To BEAUFORT + ETREE-WAMIN to see O.C. Adj of Devons re taking over clothing at BERLENCOURT Baths. To WARLUS to see OC D Divl Sanitary section re agreements for Baths at AGNEZ, ACHICOURT, RIVIERE + BEAUMETZ.	
	8th		To BERLENCOURT Baths. To La Ble HdQrs to see Staff Capt. re alterations required to Baths at BERLENCOURT, + supply of a stoker required there. To AVESNES to arrange for supply	

Army Form C. 2118.

WAR DIARY
or
INTELLIGENCE SUMMARY
(Erase heading not required.)

Place	Date	Hour	Summary of Events and Information	Remarks and references to Appendices
Le CAUROY	Nov. 1916	9th (Continued)	of clean linen at BERLENCOURT Baths - after consultation with MO i/c to SOMBRIN Baths in course of construction.	
	10th		Lorry to ABBEVILLE. Made arrangements for distributing lectures into villages. Attended 3 lectures at Corps Med Schools. To BERLENCOURT to consult with Engineer re accommodation for 2nd Bath at to Baths. To OPPY AVERGNY with Engineer's Representative.	
	11th		Inspected 43 Bde. H Qrs. etc. at LIENCOURT. (T.M Batt, M.G.Co, H.Qrs AWR.) Office work.	
	12th		To BERLENCOURT Baths & PREVENT Laundry. Office work.	
	13th		Inspected GRAND RULLECOURT SOMBRIN with DADMS. To AVESNES. Col Dunlop at GRAND RULLECOURT.	
	14th		Lectured at Corps Med Schools. To New Laundry at PREVENT. Office work. To Laundry at AVESNES. Lorry to GRAND RULLECOURT	
	15th		Pte. BISHOP 2250 on leave. Lectured at Corps Med Schools. Pte Graham 767 & Archibald (P.110) inspected BEAUDRICOURT. Offy. NERGNY Baths at SOMBRIN. Lorry shifting stores from old laundry at AVESNES to Laundry AVESNES with DADMS. New laundry at PREVENT (3 days. 15th-18th)	
	16th		Pte SMITH M99 to be kept without extra fat attached to his unit. — to Hauteville Unit 4 Hygiene men to supervise sanitation of the village. Lectured at Div: Schools — Inspected 43 Bde. H Qrs, 4 T.M. Batt, M.G.Cy, a SLI with DADMS. Inspected SARS-le-Bois DENIERS.	

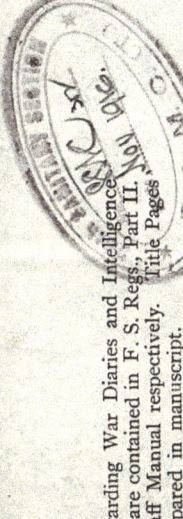

WAR DIARY or INTELLIGENCE SUMMARY

Army Form C. 2118.

Place	Date	Hour	Summary of Events and Information	Remarks and references to Appendices
Le Cauroy	November 17.		Attended lectures at Corps. Med. Schools with ADMS. Office work.	Pte Beard evacuated sick — date n.k. known.
	18.		Inspected 10 DLI at SIBIVILLE + 2 Coys KOYLI at SERICOURT with DADMS. Attended Medical Conference at VI Corps H.Qrs. To PREVENT Laundry Office work. To AGNES. Inspected sanitation of Le Cauroy.	
	19.		Inspected Divl Schools at GRAND RULLECOURT. To SOMBRIN Baths. Inspected sanitation of 8 KRRC & RB.	
	20.		Officer undisposed. DADMS inspected 11th King's Liverpools at BUNEVILLE, + 6 DCLI + 89 MG Coy RE's at MONCHEAUX and MONT-EN-TERNOIS.	
	21.		Inspected sanitation of 9 RB at BEAUDRICOURT, OPPY, and 5 KSLI at VERGNY. To Baths at OPPY. Pte GORDON 767 evacuated sick.	
	22.		Discussed laundry matters with ADMS. 9/4 HEATHER to Divl Schools GRAND RULLECOURT re alterations to sanitary erections. To PREVENT laundry to baths at SOMBRIN.	
	23.		To Corps Hd Qrs. with ADMS re Clayton Disinfector. Wt ADMS to PREVENT laundry re drainage.	
	24.		OPPY, BERLENCOURT, HOUVIN-HOUVIGNEUL and SERICOURT. DADMS inspected Le Cauroy. Inspected sanitary exhibition at BERLENCOURT. Lorry to SOMBRIN & PREVENT with clean + dirty linen.	
	25.		Office work. To SERICOURT with Interpreter re threshing of corn in Baths adjacent to Baths.	
	26.			

Army Form C. 2118.

WAR DIARY
or
INTELLIGENCE SUMMARY

(Erase heading not required.)

Place	Date 1916	Hour	Summary of Events and Information	Remarks and references to Appendices
Le CAUROY	Nov 27		Inspected sanitation of Le CAUROY. Reports to various Units. Lorry to PREVENT Laundry + Refilling Point	
	Nov 28		To GRAND RULLECOURT – Inspected sanitation of Divl Schools with acting DADMS. Also inspected 8 KRRC + 8 RB. Lorry to Sombrin Btn + PREVENT.	
	Nov 29		Inspected sanitation of 43 Bde H. Qrs, 43 M.G. Coy, 43 TMBatt, + 6 S.L.I. at HOUVIN-HOUVIGNEUL. Visited Baths at 43 Bde Hd Qrs. Lorry to PREVENT, SOMBRIN + BERNEVILLE.	
	Nov 30		Lorry to Workshops. No ambul. Dr. DENNISON, E.T. MT. A.S.C. reported from Mob Supply Col— Inspected sanitation of BERNEVILLE with ADMS.	

Dorothy Pike
Col.
ACB Sanitary Section
XVII (Light) Division

2449 Wt. W14957/M90 750,000 1/16 J.B.C. & A. Forms/C.2118/12.

140/1903
Vol 20

Dec 1916

25th Sanitary Section. 14th Div.

War Diary.

For period — December 1 to 31, 1916.

COMMITTEE FOR THE
MEDICAL HISTORY OF THE WAR
Date 31 JAN. 1917

Army Form C. 2118.

WAR DIARY
or
INTELLIGENCE SUMMARY

(Erase heading not required.)

Place	Date 1916	Hour	Summary of Events and Information	Remarks and references to Appendices
Le CAUROY.	Dec 1.		Inspected sanitation of 11th Kings Liverpools. Visited Baths at OPPY & SOMBRIN.	
	2.		Inspected sanitation of 10th D.L.I. at SIBIVILLE - with D.A.D.M.S. D. MULLCHAP. U.S. on leave to England.	
	3.		Inspected sanitation of Le CAUROY - Office work. Sent Sgt HEATHER to N Corps Med. Schools.	
			Came Pioneer Sgt. 11th Kings Liverpool Regiment.	
	4.		Inspected 6th KOYLI at Mont-en-Ternois & BUNEVILLE. Office work.	
	5.		Inspected 26th Mobile Vet Section at Mont. JOIE FERME - sent report to I.C.	
			P/o HATTON on leave to England.	
	6.		Inspected sanitation of 6 DCLI at MONCHEAUX.	
	7.		DADMS inspected sanitation of Le CAUROY. Inspected sanitation of 8 RB + DWI Schools	
			at GRAND RULLECOURT - also 8 KRRC.	
	8.		Inspected sanitation of 7 KRRC at SOMBRIN with DADMS. M.D.	
			To FLIEVRES & HESDIN with DADMS re proposed laundry.	
			To X/N Divl. Sub/y Column re washing machine mangle.	
	9.		DADMS inspected LIENCOURT.	
	10.		Visited 3rd Army Sanitation School Exhibition with ADMS + DADMS.	
			Tested section attached men's gas Respirators in Gas Chamber.	

WAR DIARY or INTELLIGENCE SUMMARY

Army Form C. 2118.

Place	Date 1916	Hour	Summary of Events and Information	Remarks and references to Appendices
LE CAUROY (continued)	Dec 11		Inspected sanitation of 10 DLI at SIBVILLE & 9 RB at GRAND RULLECOURT. Sanitary Exhibition at LIGNEREUIL & Baths at TINCBRIN with DADMS - DADMS (sanitary) 1st Army.	
	12		Lectured at VI Corps Med. Schools. Inspected sanitation of Artillery 3rd Army. A/C Bakery &c	
	13		46 Bde RFA at ETREE WAMIN — interviewed OC. Inspected sanitation of 9 RB at AUDRUICQ. Lectured at VI Corps Med Schools. LIGNEREUIL.	
	14		Reported to ADMS. Office work.	
	15		Inspected sanitation of DAC at WERGNY — reported to ADMS. Visited BERLENCOURT re billeting. To BEAUDRICOURT re 2 cases of Diphtheria in 17 Bde RFA — saw MO. To WARLUS hope OC to WN Sam. Pce re taking over. Pte CRULEY on leave	
	16		Inspected sanitation of Le Cauroy. Attended Conference of DAsDMS + D'sC Sanitary Sections at Army HdQrs ST POL. Handed over to Major Tyndale DADMS (San) 3rd Army.	
	17		Attended Corps Conference with ADMS. Office work.	
	18		To WARLUS hope OC to Div Sam Pce.	
	19		At Lechin Farm from Le Cauroy to WARLUS.	
WARLUS	20		Inspected sanitation of BERNEVILLE, SIMENCOURT.	
	21		Prepared lecture notes. Office work. To Capt HdQrs with DADMS. Cpl. SMITH on leave.	
	22		Interviewed T.M. BERNEVILLE. Inspected BEAUMETZ & reported to ADMS on insanitary conditions. Left on 1st Division.	

WAR DIARY or INTELLIGENCE SUMMARY

Army Form C. 2118.

(Erase heading not required.)

Place	Date	Hour	Summary of Events and Information	Remarks and references to Appendices
WARLUS (continued)	Dec 23.		Inspected sanitation of RIVIERE, GROSVILLE, etc. — reported on insanitary conditions left by 17th Division.	
	24.		Visited front line trenches in "E" Sector led by 7KRRC with ADMS. MO. Reference to Manure heaps.	
	25.		To BERNEVILLE, SIMENCOURT, GOUY with DDMS VI Corps ADMS. Saw Town Majors with reference to Manure heaps.	
			Reviewed Town Majors of GOUY, FOSSEUX, BARLY — selected with them, sites for Manure dumps.	
	26.		Visited Town Majors of BERNEVILLE, SIMENCOURT, BARLY with ADMS re manure dumps & VI Corps Sanitation orders. In afternoon to FOSSEUX on similar errand.	
	27.		To BEAUMETZ, MONCHIET on sanitary inspection — To FOSSEUX, BARLY.	
	28.		To St. POL to lecture at 3rd Army School. Lorry to Beaumetz with stores.	
	29.		Paid men. Office work. To Doulens to purchase stores.	
	30.		To BEAUMETZ to approve site chosen for manure dump. To MONCHIET re manure dump & sites for latrines, cookhouses etc. at Hutments. To Town Major Gouy re dike. To T.M. Berneville re change of site for manure dump following complaint from owner of present site.	
	31.		To BEAUMETZ re latrine sites for latrines, cookhouses, etc. To MONCHIET to inspect sites of outer cookhouses, latrines etc. in Village. To BERNEVILLE to inspect new site for manure dump.	

140/943.

14th Ds

25th Sanitary Section.

COMMITTEE FOR THE
MEDICAL HISTORY OF THE WAR
Date 13 MAR 1917

14.

25" Sanity C[?]
Vol 21
Army Form C. 2118.

WAR DIARY
or
INTELLIGENCE SUMMARY.
(Erase heading not required.)

Instructions regarding War Diaries and Intelligence Summaries are contained in F.S. Regs. Part II. and the Staff Manual respectively. Title pages will be prepared in manuscript.

25th SANITARY SECTION
No. ......
Date Jan. 1917
R.A.M.C. (T.)

Place	Date 1917	Hour	Summary of Events and Information	Remarks and references to Appendices
WARLUS	Jan 1		Inspected BEAUMETZ and selected sites for cookhouses, latrines, ablution benches, etc. Arranged with Town Major as to locating sites on maps and furnishing information to A.A. & Q.M.G. Inspected part of GOUY in same way.	
	2.		To BERNEVILLE, BEAUMETZ and SIMENCOURT with D.M.S. VI Corps to choose sites for accommodation of extra wounded. To SIMENCOURT re Washing Machines. To Divisional Schools GRAND RULLECOURT re elimination of water. To Laundry AVESNES re repairs necessary etc. Lorry to AVESNES for inspection.	
	3.		To Town Major and G.M.O. BERNEVILLE. Gave form "M.P" bodegas for NCO at Manure Dump. Arranged with latter for supply of clean clothing to be sent in afternoon. Arranged for disinfection of 1500 blankets for N.T.L.9. Completed siting of cookhouses etc. at GOUY. Attended lecture models from VI Corps school at Lignereuil. Saw Corps S.R.E's. re work at Divisional Laundry and repairs to Drying Room. Interviewed C.R.E. with reference to tanks for Creol sterilization of dirty clothing. Telephoned in answer to D.D.M.S. VI Corps re shield of Standard latrine required by Corps Engineers. Took shields and models of other urinals to Corps HdQrs. Interview with D.D.M.S. followed by interview with C.R.E. Left shields with latter to be copied and returned. Arranged with P.P.M.S. system for dumping manure at the various village dumps. Sketched plan shewing by diagram how this should be carried out and gave details for distribution to Town Majors. Lorry to Rifling Point and Berneville Baths with clean clothing.	
	4.		Arranged distribution of 21 men obtained from Battalions allotting 5 each to BEAUMETZ, MONCHIET, RIVIÈRE, GOUY, and one to BERNEVILLE. To Corps HdQrs to see D.A.Q.M.G. with reference to supply of biscuit-boxes for latrine seats. Arranged matter satisfactorily. To Corps Engineers with plan for ablution bench and standard type of latrine seat, single and triple, as models to be copied. To Divisional Laundry AVESNES to inspect progress of work &c. To BERNEVILLE to see late O.C. Baths with reference to	

Army Form C. 2118.

WAR DIARY
or
INTELLIGENCE SUMMARY.
(Erase heading not required.)

Place	Date	Hour	Summary of Events and Information	Remarks and references to Appendices
WARLUS	Jan 4. 1917		Clothing stores. Had cancellation of D.R.O. 2078 with reference to biscuit boxes for latrine seats rescinded and agreed upon new form of original order. Gave instructions for biscuit boxes to be collected by me at Repelling Points. Lorry to R.E. Park, LARBRET and Divisional Laundry AVESNES.	
	5.		To RIVIERE to select sites for cookhouses, latrines, etc. Saw D.A.Q.M.G. with reference to disposal of sanitary maps of the village. Despatched clean clothing to Divisional schools, GRAND RULLECOURT. Lorry to Repelling Point. Office work.	
	6.		Lorry to VI Corps Head Quarters NOEUX VION with model Atkestar Bench for DDMS, and to GOUY for coal. Despatched clean clothing to BERNEVILLE Baths. To Q. Office re Foden Lorry. Saw C.R.E. with reference to drying shed required at SIMENCOURT. To BERNEVILLE to stop disinfestion of blankets by Foden Lorry and arranged programme of its work for next few days. To SIMENCOURT to select sites for cookhouses, etc. with Town Major. Took Assistant C.R.E. to Laundry AVESNES and arranged for work necessary to put drying room into proper repair.	
	7.		Selected sites for cookhouses etc at BERNEVILLE with Town Major. To Major AVESNES re Billeting certificate for Laundry. To Laundry to inspect progress of improvements being carried out by R.E. To Q. Office re Foden lorry and extra men required at RIVIERE, and A.C.O and fatigue at DAINVILLE, being taken over from O.C Division.	
	8.		Conference at Q Office on Baths and laundries with A.A.Q.M.G, DADMS, DADOS and Supt. Shepherd. To 41st and 43rd Brigade H.Q.s with D.A.D.M.S; thence to travellers and Amiens with reference to Laundry	

Army Form C. 2118.

WAR DIARY
or
INTELLIGENCE SUMMARY.
(Erase heading not required.)

Instructions regarding War Diaries and Intelligence Summaries are contained in F. S. Regs., Part II. and the Staff Manual respectively. Title pages will be prepared in manuscript.

Place	Date 1917	Hour	Summary of Events and Information	Remarks and references to Appendices
WARLUS	Jan: 8.		Facilities. Capt Shepherd took over Baths and Laundries. Lorry to Refilling Point. Private Pennison on leave to England.	
	9.		Lorry to Refilling Point. L/Cpl Smith transferred from GOUY to DAINVILLE to take charge of sanitation of the latter village. Five fatigue men also transferred.	
	10.		To ACHICOURT, AGNY and WAILLY for inspection of villages. Two reinforcements arrived (Pte Brown, No.1361 and Pte Sanders 1368). Office work.	
	11.		Lectured at H.Q. W. Pol. Lorry to de Fermont with clothing for Baths.	
	12.		Officer on leave to England. Lorry to Refilling Point and Forsuns with stores.	
	22.		Officer returned from leave. Office work.	
	23.		Inspected sanitation of WARLUS with A.D.M.S. – Office work.	
	24.		To BERNEVILLE to inspect sites of new latrines, cookhouses, &c. with new Town Major.	
	25.		To MONCHIET re siting of cookhouses, etc. Also selected sites for same in WARLUS with Town Major.	
	26.		Lectured on Field Sanitation at 3rd Army Headquarters.	
	27.		To St POL to arrange with D.A.D.M.S. (Sanitation) 3rd Army for building Exhibition of Sanitary apparatus at School of Sanitation St POL. To GOUY to select additional site for cookhouses etc. with Town Major.	
	28		To DAINVILLE to select sites for cookhouses etc. with Town Major. To AVESNES-le-COMTE to draw money to pay section & for necessary materials for section workshop.	

WAR DIARY
or
INTELLIGENCE SUMMARY.

Army Form C. 2118.

Place	Date	Hour	Summary of Events and Information	Remarks and references to Appendices
WARLUS	Jan 29 1917		To SIMENCOURT to select sites for cookhouses etc. To Town Major BERNEVILLE re discrepancies in reports as to cookhouses etc. Paid men.	
	30		To MONCHIET to oil cookhouses etc. for additional 8,000 troops. Submitted model latrine (10 seater) and washing machine for inspection by A.A. & Q.M.G.	
	31		Inspected sanitation of WARLUS.	

E Murphy Lieut
W/-
OC 25 San Sec
XVII (Light) Division

Feb 10/ 1917

Confidential

War Diary

of

O.C. 2:5th Sanitary Section

for

month of February.

Army Form C. 2118.

WAR DIARY
or
INTELLIGENCE SUMMARY.
(Erase heading not required.)

Instructions regarding War Diaries and Intelligence Summaries are contained in F. S. Regs., Part II. and the Staff Manual respectively. Title pages will be prepared in manuscript.

Place	Date	Hour	Summary of Events and Information	Remarks and references to Appendices
WARLUS	1917 Feb. 1.		Officer indisposed. Office work.	
	2.		Officer indisposed. Office work. Arranged re-distribution of sub-sections following change in Divisional area. Saw A.A & Q.M.G. with reference to withdrawal and redistribution of sanitary fatigues allotted to various villages. Also saw A.A. of Q.M.G. and C.R.E. and arranged for 4 Sappers for temporary duty in Sanitary Section Workshop.	
	3.		Officer indisposed. Office work.	
	4.		Sanitary inspection of BERNEVILLE.	
	5.		To Amiens for materials required in Workshop.	
	6.		To SIMENCOURT to select fresh sites in connection with new hutting.	
	7.		To AYESNES Laundry and Field Cashier. To BARLY re Baths. Brought C.R.E. old French boiler for experimental purposes in washing point. Staff-Sergt. Tuller on leave to England.	2392 Sergt. Tuller N on leave to England
	8.		To RONVILLE with A.D.M.S. in reference to sanitation of caves.	
	9.		To ABBEVILLE with D.A.D.M.S. with reference to new Laundry arrangements.	
	10.		To ST POL to lecture at School of Sanitation. L/Corpl. CLEAL T.A. admitted to Hospital sick.	
	11.		To DAINVILLE to pay Laundry account. To RONVILLE re sanitation of caves.	
	12.		To C.E. VII Corps re construction of sanitary apparatus for caves	
	13.		To SOMBRIN to inspect sanitation of 4th H.R.C. Cadets (1 Company + Headquarters). Office work.	

Army Form C. 2118.

WAR DIARY
or
INTELLIGENCE SUMMARY.

(Erase heading not required.)

Place	Date 1917	Hour	Summary of Events and Information	Remarks and references to Appendices
WARLUS	Feb. 14th		Office work. To Corps Engineers to arrange for supply of latrine seats to be made for my workshops. Saw A.A.D.M.S. re sanitation of SIMENCOURT. Arranged for village to be furnished forthwith and wired Corps Engineers VII Corps re material. To DOULLENS for materials and to meet Baths Officer.	
	16.		To RONVILLE re sanitation of caves. Office work.	
	17.		Sanitary inspection of WARLUS.	
	18.		Sanitary inspection of DAINVILLE.	
	19.		To VII Corps Parks re form of latrine for use in Corps area. To BAIRLY with A.D.M.S.	
	20.		To DAINVILLE with A.D.M.S. to inspect premises occupied by Brigade Canteen with a view to fitting them up as Collecting Post for wounded. Handed over sanitary care of WARLUS to O.C. 3rd Division Sanitary Section.	
	21.		Sanitary inspection of BERNEVILLE.	
	22.		To ABBEVILLE with O.C. Baths & Laundries. Generally inspected Laundry arrangements	
	23.		To ST POL to coline at 3rd Army School of Sanitation. 2/Lt. CLEAL T.A. returned from hospital	

PROMOTIONS:—

No.	Rank	Name	Promoted to	With effect from
2392	Sergt.	Hassell W	Acting Staff-Sergt. (without extra pay)	24-2-17
2372	Cpl (Act/Sergt)	Heather N	Acting Staff-Sergt. (without extra pay)	24-2-17

WAR DIARY
or
INTELLIGENCE SUMMARY.

Army Form C. 2118.

(Erase heading not required.)

Place	Date 1917	Hour	Summary of Events and Information	Remarks and references to Appendices
WARLUS	Feb. 23		PROMOTIONS (continued)	

No.	Rank	Name	Promoted to.	with effect from
2277	Pte (Act/Cpl)	Smith, H.	To the vacant rank of T/Cpl. with pay	24-2-17
2349	Pte (Act. L/Cpl.)	Clark, W.T.	Acting Corpl. (without extra pay)	24-2-17
2863	do.	Marshall, G.	do.	do.
3242	do.	Cropper, J.E.	do.	do.
4384	Pte.	Hatton, J.	} Acting L/Cpls (without extra pay)	24-2-17
3152	Pte.	Huggins, W.E.		do.

		24	Consultation with Corps Engineers VII Corps re sanitation of XIV Division area. Inspected sanitation of FONVILLE. Saw Town Major re same.	
		25	Sanitary inspection of BERNEVILLE road A.D.M.S. To BARLY and FOSSEUX with A.D.M.S. Drew money from Field Cashier to pay Section.	
		26	To SIMENCOURT. Saw Town Major re Manure Dumps. Also saw Town Major of 46th Division with reference to relief of 25th Sanitary Sectn. on that Division taking over charge of the village. To BARLY with A.D.M.S.	
		27	Office work. Inspection of Headquarters sanitation. Inspected DAINVILLE with A.D.M.S. Paid men	
		28	To SIMENCOURT to see O.C. 235 R.E. with reference to construction of sanitary appliances in BERNEVILLE. To 42nd and 43rd Brigade Headquarters ARRAS, and	

WAR DIARY or INTELLIGENCE SUMMARY

Army Form C. 2118.

Place	Date	Hour	Summary of Events and Information	Remarks and references to Appendices
WARLUS	1917 Feb. 28		To inspect cases and see O.C. Bases. Arranged for withdrawal of SIMENCOURT Sub-Section with effect 1st March. DISTRIBUTION:- (March 1st/1917)	

PLACE	Officers	O.R.
WARLUS	1	8
BERNEVILLE		4
DAINVILLE		4
ARRAS		3
RONVILLE		3
VI CORPS H.Q.		1
BARLY		1
IN HOSPITAL, ENGLAND.		1

Ethor W Ryh
Capt.
R.A.M.C.(T)
O.C. 25th Sanitary Section
XIV Division.

28th Feb. 1917.

No. 25. Sanitary Section.

14/2045.

COMMITTEE FOR THE
MEDICAL HISTORY OF THE WAR
Date 11 MAY. 1917

Army Form C. 2118.

WAR DIARY
or
INTELLIGENCE SUMMARY.
(Erase heading not required.)

Place	Date 1917	Hour	Summary of Events and Information	Remarks and references to Appendices
WARLUS	March 1		Inspected Sanitation in front line Rufford (2. H Sector) opposite ARRAS - RONVILLE) with A.D.M.S. Creosol drums under lavseats. Thos or less flyproof, but lids not automatic generally found open. Latrines much too scattered & few in number. Sent Sergt. FILKINS from VI Corps H.Q. Typhoid to C.C. Caves to look after Sanitation below ground. WORKSHOP: Blenwellets notice board & Co. Baths. E.S. Wagn to DAINVILLE for Stores	
	2		To SIMENCOURT to see Town Majors. Care of village handed back to XIV Div. Sant Sects Sect. Las therefore been returned to duty there. To RONVILLE to advise C.C. Caves with ref. to treatment of well water. Water is of good quality - but contains suspended chalk & promises 1 scoop at a time for 100 feet. + GMOU Rode to SIMENCOURT & BERNEVILLE with A.D.M.S & interviewed Town Majors with ref. to daily Sanitary inspection of the villages. To DAINVILLE - ditto. Arranged to draw up Sanitary Orders for villages. Sent Staff Sergt. HEATHER & 5others to BIPOL to meet Sanitary Exhibition at III Army School of Sanitation.	
	3		WORKSHOP: Arranged for G.S. Wagn to draw notes (similar to) from PAULTY. 4 Box Latrines to Wircal for D.H.Q. Attached 4/c CLEAR & 6prot to Q. Office to keep in process of work.	

Army Form C. 2118.

WAR DIARY
or
INTELLIGENCE SUMMARY.
(Erase heading not required.)

Instructions regarding War Diaries and Intelligence Summaries are contained in F.S. Regs., Part II. and the Staff Manual respectively. Title pages will be prepared in manuscript.

Place	Date 1917	Hour	Summary of Events and Information	Remarks and references to Appendices
WARLUS	March 4		Drew up with ADMS Sanitary Orders. These the printed in Q Offices & distributed to Town Majors for issue to O'sC units taking up quarters in village. O'sC units to be responsible that the Regulations are carried out. NOTE: 2372 Corpl. (acting Staff Sergeant) N. HEATHER was awarded the MILITARY MEDAL in Dec. last for courage in carrying on with his duties after having been temporarily buried as a result of heavy shell fire in the Ramparts at YPRES on (or about) 23 Sept. 1915 - & for continuous good work since arriving with the Sectn in France MAY 1915. WORKSHOP: G.S. Wagon & BAULTY for timber &c. 14 single seat & 1 4-seat Latrines for Town Majors RONVILLE (7 & arrivals) 3 new lids for Latrines in BERNEVILLE	
	5		To BERNEVILLE & interview Town Major Sanitary officer. Inspected Officers' Encampment. To RONVILLE & inspect Caves occupied by 3 Companies (500 men) 1st KOYLI. Found atmosphere slightly heavy & damp, but not very bad. Some smoke was due to fire which had been lit at the Windward end of Caves. The sanitation was very satisfactory. No odour at all in Latrines or near Urinals. Cookhouses clean & working well. Required: 40 Brule tube. Heavy oil for Urinals. Latrine paper. Sergt. FILKINS reported sick. Sent to 42nd F.A. He had instructed Sanitary Squad in Caves & are capable of carrying out their duties under supervision of a corpl. in charge.	Ellis

Army Form C. 2118.

WAR DIARY
or
INTELLIGENCE SUMMARY.
(Erase heading not required.)

Instructions regarding War Diaries and Intelligence Summaries are contained in F. S. Regs., Part II. and the Staff Manual respectively. Title pages will be prepared in manuscript.

Place	Date	Hour	Summary of Events and Information	Remarks and references to Appendices
WARLUS	March 1917 5 (cont)		WORKSHOP. 1 10-seat latrine to 14 DHQ 1 5-seat " " To 6 urinals to DAINVILLE G.S. Wagon to DAINVILLE for timber.	
	6.		Saw VII Corps R.E. Obtained authority to draw materials to & discussed flyproof kitchens. He agreed to flyproof larders in each case. Made sanitary inspection of SIMENCOURT with Town Major & S.M.O. Sent to Grande RULLECOURT for Sub Schools Huts sprayed with formalin after infectious cases. WORKSHOP: 6 single latrines to 46 Bde RFA 3. 4-seater " " to RONVILLE District Rounds to BERNEVILLE G.S. Wagon with stores to DAINVILLE & RONVILLE	
	7		To DUISANS to discuss matters with Capt. JURY O.C. 32nd San. Sec. 15-A Div. Inspected sanitation in front line & supports in part of "H" LEFT & part of "H" RIGHT with M.O's of 9.2.KRRC & 10th DLI. Some attempt at flyproofing latrines - but not altogether satisfactory - insufficiency of flyproofing latrines. Arranged with MO's to make latrines in Workshop send up. Spoke with Director Remarks. Workshop. 14 single seater latrines to SIMENCOURT 1 10- " " " DAINVILLE 4- " " " RONVILLE G.S. Wagon trips to DAINVILLE/RONVILLE/SIMENCOURT	

Army Form C. 2118.

WAR DIARY
or
INTELLIGENCE SUMMARY.
(Erase heading not required.)

Instructions regarding War Diaries and Intelligence Summaries are contained in F.S. Regs., Part II. and the Staff Manual respectively. Title pages will be prepared in manuscript.

Place	Date 1917	Hour	Summary of Events and Information	Remarks and references to Appendices
WARLUS	MARCH 8		Inspected & advised on drainage & treatment of waste water at & the DAINVILLE Sanitation at DAINVILLE & drew T.M's attention to bad conditions of 3rd Army Survey Co. for short stay. Workshop: 2 4-Seater Latrines & RONVILLE 38 Notice Boards	
	9		Finished inspection of DAINVILLE & inspected Sanitation Latrines at RONVILLE with A.D.M.S. Arrangements quite satisfactory. Workshop: 1 10-Seat Latrine & DAINVILLE 2 4 " " " 6 " RONVILLE Note: Lorry returned from Workshop	
	10		Discussed front line Sanitation with A.D.M.S. & established flyproof single latrine made of iron buckets – Have to be made in required numbers in workshop & sent up. Suggested pits should be dug alongside each bucket latrine for use in sudden evacuations of troops, when bucket accommodation might not be sufficient. Inspected Sanitation at 3rd Base Depot, GRANDE RULLECOURT. Satisfactory except for latrines which M.R.E. disregarding the plans given him, had wrongly constructed. They are not flyproof & the buckets are too low, with no wire baffles attached & fronts of seats which are fouled with urine in consequence. Workshop: 2 4-Seat Latrines & RONVILLE 1 5 " " " DAINVILLE 22 Notice Boards & RONVILLE	

Army Form C. 2118.

WAR DIARY
or
INTELLIGENCE SUMMARY.
(Erase heading not required.)

Instructions regarding War Diaries and Intelligence Summaries are contained in F. S. Regs., Part II. and the Staff Manual respectively. Title pages will be prepared in manuscript.

Place	Date 1917	Hour	Summary of Events and Information	Remarks and references to Appendices
WARLUS	MARCH 11		Inspected Sanitation at BERNEVILLE. Report N.A.D. Report to ADMS on alterations required to on water supply in BERNEVILLE. Inspected Sanitation at Div. H.Q. & reported to Camp Commandant unsatisfactory conditions. Workshop: 1 10-Seat Latrine + BERNEVILLE. 1 Single. " "	
	12		Inspected R.A.P's in CAVES at RONVILLE with A.D.M.S. Good Conduct badges awarded to L/c Smith E.W., L/c Marshall H., L/c Hatton. Ptes. Rogers, Bishop, Flint.	
	13		To ARRAS with ADMS & discussed Sanitation of R.A.P's in Caves with Lieut + O.C. 44th F.A. To DRS at BARLY with ADMS re disinfection of Blankets by Clayton "Disinfector".	
	14		To SIMENCOURT. Saw G.M.O. with reference to forming active Latrines in all infectious cases. To O.C. Caves RONVILLE re preparing pits for Latrines in R.A.P's. Sergt FILKINS returned from Hospital. Workshops: 2 4-Seat Latrines + RONVILLE.	
	15		To Corps HQ with ADMS re Flyproof Latrines & Flyproof Kitchens. The Corps are building kitchens in my area & Latrines & battalion trenches &c. According to army orders latrines &c are to be rendered flyproof after much argument all I can get Corps to agree to is Flyproof/Ladders - but even this is only a promise for the future. To DUISANS XV DIV. SAN. SEC. Inspected Refuse Dump & Incinerator & Special Latrines for Carrying 2 fall water cases up trenches. Shall copy.	

A5834 Wt. W4973/M687 750,000 8/16 D.D. & L. Ltd. Forms/C.2118/13.

WAR DIARY or INTELLIGENCE SUMMARY

Army Form C. 2118.

(Erase heading not required.)

Place	Date 1917	Hour	Summary of Events and Information	Remarks and references to Appendices
WARLUS	March 15 (cont)		Workshop: 15 Notice Boards to DAINVILLE	
	16		To DAINVILLE to arrange billets for 8 additional Salvage Men to assist in erecting latrines & making 22 men in all. This large number is necessary till horse transport for refuse is not available & is dependent for military reasons.	
			Inspected Sanitation at BERNEVILLE with Tn Major Sanitary Officer. Artillery had created a Lorse in pit dug for latrines. Requested T.M. to instruct them to move it on any fresh pit.	
			Workshop: 20 Officers latrines to DAINVILLE	
	17		Work DADMS (San) 3rd Army re treatment of horse thanures which should be stacked regn	
			Inspected Baths at SOMBRIN & intimated NCO i/c in treatment of horse thanures which should be stacked regn water.	
			Discussed matters with T.M. & arranged Head Sanitary NCO to report of take charge of Sanitation	
			fatigues in village.	
			Workshop: 2 10-seat latrines to BERNEVILLE	
			17 double urinal buckets "	
			4 Cutting-up boards to Div Schools	
	18		Sent Sergt. FIRMINS to GRANDE RULLECOURT to supervise Sanitation.	
			To VII Corps H.Q. (DDMS) with ADMS re infectious cases at FOSSEUX.	
			Sent Corpl. HOLLIS & L/C. MARSHALL to SOMBRIN to supervise Sanitation.	
			Workshop: 1 10-seat latrine to BERNEVILLE	
			20 Officers latrines to DAINVILLE	

Army Form C. 2118.

WAR DIARY
or
INTELLIGENCE SUMMARY.
(Erase heading not required.)

Instructions regarding War Diaries and Intelligence Summaries are contained in F. S. Regs., Part II. and the Staff Manual respectively. Title pages will be prepared in manuscript.

Place	Date 1917	Hour	Summary of Events and Information	Remarks and references to Appendices
WARLUS	March 19		To ABBEVILLE & purchase materials for section & utils for Cairn.	
			Workshop: 1 10-seat latrine to BERNEVILLE	
			2 Officers latrines & further Orders to Bn. H.Q.	
			31 Notice boards in German paint "WOUNDED" with direction arrow & ADMS " " of entering "	
	20		To inspect condition of captured German trenches with ADMS & suggest means of entering sanitation in captured areas.	
			Visited 42nd & 43rd Bde. H.Q. & arranged with Staff Capts. & send up NCO to each to direct work of Divisional Sanitary Squads. Work under forward Battalion M.O's.	
			Arranged stand up at over number of single line latrines & 3 man pits in selected sites — that permanent bucket latrines be forward complete when position becomes more settled	
			Arranged to send forward box latrines as position is advanced from time to time.	
			Sent Staff Sergt FULLER to 43rd Bde. to work & find.	
			Workshop: 3 Officers latrines 873 + Bae	
			10 Means	
			6 Notice Boards	
	21		Took Sergt. FILKINS & 42nd Bae for trench duty, & arranged duties.	
			Paid Section attached men.	
			100 Workshop: 1 Three' latrine Officers & Nurses to BERNEVILLE	

Army Form C. 2118.

Instructions regarding War Diaries and Intelligence Summaries are contained in F.S. Regs., Part II. and the Staff Manual respectively. Title pages will be prepared in manuscript.

WAR DIARY
or
INTELLIGENCE SUMMARY.
(Erase heading not required.)

Place	Date 1917	Hour	Summary of Events and Information	Remarks and references to Appendices
WARLUS	March 22		Inspected Sanitation at BOMBRIN. Demonstrated use of special drinking water carriers for use in trenches. ADMS + AA & QMG Carriers are in the form of a short detailer. Table. 6 2-gall petrol tins supplies. Workshop: 30 Officers Latrines to 43rd Divl. H.Q. 12 Water Carriers for Trench Warfare. A/13dd. H.Q. 13 orders. 20 Notice Boards for ditto.	
	23		Lectured on Field Sanitation at 3rd Army School of Sanitation. Workshop: 1 Trench Latrine & 1 Water Carrier to 3rd Army School of Sanitation St. POL	
	24		Inspected Sanitation at DAINVILLE. Sergt FILLINS evacuated to 43 C.C.S. Rheumatic Fever.	
	25		Sited Cookhouse, Latrines, &c. for new Artillery Camp at BERNEVILLE. To Corps H.Q. re malaria. Capt HOLLIS & 2/Lt MARSHALL moved back to SIMENCOURT on re-taking over the village. Pte BROWN to BERNEVILLE. Workshop: 6 Latrines 6 Urinals to RONVILLE. 9 Notice Boards " "	
	26		Conference of DADsMS + O.C. San Secs. at 3rd Army H.Q. Workshop: 1 10-seat Latrine to BERNEVILLE 6 Urinals 28 Notice Boards to DAINVILLE + RONVILLE	S/9/.

Army Form C. 2118.

WAR DIARY
or
INTELLIGENCE SUMMARY.
(Erase heading not required.)

Instructions regarding War Diaries and Intelligence Summaries are contained in F.S. Regs., Part II. and the Staff Manual respectively. Title pages will be prepared in manuscript.

Place	Date 1917	Hour	Summary of Events and Information	Remarks and references to Appendices
WARLUS	March 27		Inspected Sanitation at SIMENCOURT. L/C SMITH. E.V. & 2/C BROWN W.M. to 41st Bde H.Q. for trench duty on left of line. L/C MARSHALL from SIMENCOURT to 43rd Bde " " " " Pte SANDERS to SIMENCOURT " " " right " Workshops: 1 10-seat latrine to SIMENCOURT	
	28		To ABBEVILLE for materials. Workshops: 1 10-seat latrine to SIMENCOURT 14 single " " 10 Officers " " 12 double urinals " "	
	29		On Special leave to ENGLAND. Workshop: 2 4-seat latrines to RONVILLE 4 double urinals " 17 notice boards " Drew coal from GOUY for Baths DAINVILLE 20 Trench latrines to 462 Bde ARRAS	
	30		1 7-seat latrine 1 Officers " 2 Urinals 5 notice boards } to RONVILLE for A.D.S.	

Army Form C. 2118.

WAR DIARY
or
INTELLIGENCE SUMMARY.
(Erase heading not required.)

Instructions regarding War Diaries and Intelligence Summaries are contained in F.S. Regs., Part II. and the Staff Manual respectively. Title pages will be prepared in manuscript.

Place	Date	Hour	Summary of Events and Information	Remarks and references to Appendices
	1917 March			
WARLUS	31		Arrangements made for section to be withdrawn from Barastre & placed in charge of an area comprising the following villages with Headquarters at BOUY-EN-ARTOIS :	
			GOUY — Staff Sergt HEATHER.N. Corpl CROPPER, Ptes FLINT, KEITH, BISHOP, PALMER, SAUNDERS	
			ACHICOURT } Staff Sergt FULLER	
			AGNY } L/c MARSHALL H.J.	
			BEAUMETZ.. L/c SMITH V. L/c BROWN	
			MONCHIET.. Corpl. EYRE	
			SIMENCOURT Corpl HOLLIS Pte ROGERS	
			BAVINCOURT L/c HUGGINS	
			SAULTY } Staff Sergt HAXELL	
			LARBRET } Corpl. CLARK	
			LARRINER WIERS } L/c HATTON	
			DAINVILLE Sergt BAILEY L/c MACKAY	
			BERNEVILLE Corpl. SMITH H. & Corpl MARSHALL.C.	

Charles Pike
Capt.
OC. 28th Sanitary Section

A 5834 Wt. W4973/M687 750,000 8/16 D.D. & L. Ltd. Forms/C.2118/13.

www.ingramcontent.com/pod-product-compliance
Lightning Source LLC
Chambersburg PA
CBHW081421160426
43193CB00013B/2167